WILD HEART

HEART

SPIRIT

HEART

A Journey from Skeptic to Healer

SUSAN TURNER

WILD HEART
SPIRIT HEART

WILD HEART
SPIRIT HEART

ISBN 978-1-9992435-0-0 (paperback)
ISBN 978-1-9992435-1-7 (ebook)

Some names and identifying details have been changed
to protect the privacy of individuals.

Produced by Page Two
www.pagetwo.com

Cover design by Jennifer Lum and Logan Turner
Cover images by iStock; (Bird) © wwing; (Sky) © 4khz
Interior design by Jennifer Lum

www.wildheartspiritheart.com

CONTENTS

To Hazel and Giorgio
You let me see that miracles are possible and that love
never dies. You are both amazing spirit guides.
Your light is my blessing. Thank you for the roses.

To Chelsea and Logan
Two old souls who came into my life as my children.
Thank you for always giving me your love and support.

To Jeff
My unending gratitude to you for the love that keeps
our "gold ribbon" around us through this crazy,
wonderful ride called life. This journey would not
have been possible without you. xo

PROLOGUE

THE GREYNESS AND low-lying cloud closed in on the day. Droplets of rain created little trails as they made their way down the outside of the glass. My heart felt heavy and once again my mind questioned my soul.

On a ship heading north along the Pacific coast of British Columbia, I let my thoughts escape through the window. We were travelling along the Inside Passage, through a collection of islands and past a lighthouse and cottage perched on a rocky outcropping. The cottage was white with an orange roof and looked very tidy, like a storybook house. I drifted into a daydream, imagining myself living there. I could, I thought, live a solitary life far from the fast-paced material world—just live moment to moment in the ebb and flow of nature. I had a sense of romance about living in the wild, setting my spirit free to a place it belongs.

Maybe that is what it is like to die, I thought—a freedom for the spirit as it finds its way back home, released from the heaviness we often feel in our human world. I thought about how hard we fight not to die, as if dying is the enemy. But really, death is a magical release.

I had just got word of a young woman's passing. I imagined her family's grief and pain. It was hard not to feel it, as it had embraced me every time I went to bring her healing energy. I was with her for only ten days, most of which she spent in a deep sleep. During the first healing, I had the feeling that her soul was adrift. I felt as though she had already made the choice to journey onwards from the physical, and that she was between worlds much of the time. For short periods, she would open her eyes and take in the love that surrounded her. But mostly, I felt, she had decided it was time to go. Maybe she could see a clear path ahead. In the healings, we communicated primarily on a soul level, and I felt she wasn't entirely sure of the direction her life was meant to take.

So as I imagined the simplicity of life in a lighthouse, I also thought about most people's great reluctance to die. It's really not death itself that we find so unsettling—it's leaving before we've lived the life we had intended when we were born. Our soul has an intention for this lifetime, and if we live all our days without ever fulfilling that purpose, then our death will most certainly feel as if it has come too soon. To realize that your last day has arrived and that your voice, your truth, remains hidden inside—perhaps as yet undiscovered even by you—will feel like a sadness. We need to embrace life, to have the courage to live as true to our soul's calling as we can, so that when death comes, we have no regrets.

The young woman's death was a reminder that I still had much to do in my own life. Alas, being a lighthouse keeper was not part of my plan. I needed to persevere in realigning myself with my own truth—provided I had the courage to continue down that path.

INTRODUCTION

M Y JOURNEY AS a healer had begun much earlier than I had realized, during the many years I spent living in the wilderness with bears and wolves. I grew up in the remoteness of the mountains and devoted a thirty-year career to making wildlife documentaries and travelling to North America's most secluded corners. My husband, Jeff, and I worked together. We lived much of our life in wilderness settings in close company with grizzly bears, black bears, wolves, bison, caribou, and many other amazing animals.

When I was forty years old, I discovered, unexpectedly, that I could connect with healing energy from Spirit and Source. Spirit is the energy from those who have left their physical bodies, and Source is what I call the higher energies of pure, unconditional love. Some people might call this love Divine energy, Universal energy, God, or many other names. The natural world is the manifestation of Source energy on Earth, and I now believe that living much of my life in pristine wilderness paved the way for my shift to embracing the healing energy of Spirit and Source.

Helping others heal led me on a journey of discovering energy, most importantly the energy of our emotions. Over the past seventeen years I have come to understand that people are emotional-spiritual beings with many physical lives. Our emotions are powerful energies that determine not only our own health and how we experience our lives, but also the health of the planet. Our emotional energy connects us to each other, the plants, the animals, and even the Earth. I believe each of us is on a path to evolve on an emotional level to the highest realms of love and compassion. I have learned that visualizing ourselves as energy—physical, emotional, and spiritual—can help us raise our energetic vibration to a place of healing and happiness, not only for ourselves but also for the Earth.

Throughout this journey, I have been excited, inspired, scared, and unsure. I started from a place of skepticism and very little understanding, and I chose to let the truth unfold for me in its own time. I wanted to feel that what I was experiencing was fully authentic, that *I* was authentic. I took steps forward and steps back. I questioned everything from every angle, as if it were a science experiment. And the spirit world guided me along, putting opportunities in my path as I was ready, each time raising my level of understanding.

I have had the great privilege to be part of physical and emotional healings that would be considered miraculous. I have also had the great pleasure of receiving messages from Spirit that have completely changed the way I see the world and the way I live. In this book, I share stories from different healing events in which I have participated. Each person's experience took me to a higher level of understanding of what it means to truly heal, sometimes even in death. When I began this work of connecting to Spirit and helping others, my idea of healing was firmly rooted in the physical. But my experiences have shown me that sometimes the physical aspect is the least important part.

At times I was so inspired that nothing could hold me down, but on many other occasions I was filled with self-doubt. It was easy to feel alone, because I was teaching myself through practice and inspiration. It felt as if I was on a long, solitary walk in the wilderness, without a trail or a guidebook, coming upon places I had never imagined existed and having to rely on survival skills. Feeling alone made me reach out intensely for the truth, because only by my own understanding of what was true could I find my way through to my soul's light.

Since beginning this healing journey, I have wanted to discover both my truth and the truth of our existence. I didn't want to study other people's belief systems or rewrite their accumulated knowledge—I wanted this understanding to come through my own exploration. I am not interested in sounding clever or using any particular vocabulary. This field wasn't something I'd intended to study; I decided I would honour how it had unfolded before me and let it naturally lead the way, instead of forcing it.

I am not a spiritualist, although I believe in the spirit. I'm not an environmentalist, but I care deeply about the Earth and all that lives upon it. I'm not a doctor, but I have worked to help heal quite a few people. I'm not a teacher, but I think there are a few things I could talk about with some authority. I don't want to belong to any one group or be slotted into a particular segment of the population. Life means we are a part of it all. I'm just a being, living on the planet Earth, one part of the big picture, joined with all of you.

The only place I feel certain I come from is a place of love. I'm writing this book because I love deeply. This may sound a little odd. Doesn't one need more qualifications than love? But as it turns out, maybe the Beatles had it right, and it's all we need.

I am not trying to prove anything, build a case, or convert anyone to another way of being or thinking. What I realize most clearly is that the complexities beyond our physical existence are much more than anything I can begin to conceptualize at this time. But I've learned enough to feel compelled to share my experience. There's so much to celebrate in life, so much to be grateful for. And for those of you who connect with my words and feelings, I hope they can help you partake of the love and joy I've had the privilege of experiencing. We all need to heal, and my hope is that this book will help you on your own journey of healing.

I've written this book to share how I discovered my way, a way I wasn't looking for. What I found was a love I never could have imagined.

HAZEL OPENS THE DOOR

WHEN I WAS young, my dad told me that he and my mom had found me under a huckleberry bush. Maybe he wanted to avoid telling me where babies come from, but he really wasn't too far from the truth. I was born as close to nature as you could be without actually being found under a bush. We lived in a pristine country setting on the edge of the wilderness, and most of my daylight hours were spent in the outdoors. My mother believed that there were no better toys for children than sticks and tree cones, and I agreed. Rocks have filled my pockets ever since I could walk. Each small stone along the river seemed so delightful with its shape and colours; they tugged at my heartstrings to take them home.

I grew up with time and freedom and space. The magic of nature was all around me, and my mind and senses were filled with the purity of the natural world. For as long as I can remember, I've loved nature and found complete joy living as part of it. Nature, for me, is a safe and loving place. I can be myself in nature as I can in no other place. And nature fills me with the most abundant energy, a beautiful energy that reminds me why I'm glad to be alive. So no matter how my life journey winds and no matter how tricky the steps sometimes feel, the natural world always sets me free.

That's why, many years after my childhood, the little garden in front of our English cottage was so pleasing to me. It was a small sanctuary, away from the business of people and the city. There was a beautiful, gnarly apple tree and flowers going to the wild side, and a faded wooden bird feeder that brought in songbirds to delight the morning air.

On this morning, we were beginning a three-month stay in England, about to edit a film about cougars, or mountain lions. Jeff, my filmmaking partner and husband, and I had been producing nature documentaries for about twenty years. Many of our films were about grizzlies, black bears, wolves, and other large animals of the Canadian wilderness. When our daughter, Chelsea, was born, we wanted to keep our family together while we went on filmmaking trips. Filmmaking was our way of life, and the trips were filled with the most amazing experiences; I didn't want my children or myself to miss out on them.

Our first trip with Chelsea started when she was six months old. We lived on a remote coastal island, in large tents, for nearly two years, filming white-coloured black bears, called spirit bears. Our first trip with our son, Logan, began when he was five months old. We lived on the northern plains of western Canada, filming wolves and buffalo. So my children, in turn, grew up with a great understanding, respect, and love for the natural world.

But for about three months of every year we lived and edited in England, where the children could experience the culture and excitement of Bristol and London. We loved the theatre and all the different cuisines, and we made a great group of friends, some of whom became like a second family to us. Our life in the wilderness and the city was a delightful mix of animals and people.

Jeff left first thing in the morning to go into the editing suite at the BBC, while I stayed at home with the kids so they could do their school work. Chelsea was now eleven years old and Logan was seven. They both took their schooling by correspondence. We would work on their main lessons in the morning and then all meet in the editing room for the afternoon, where I would help with the editing while Chelsea and Logan finished their school work.

Thankfully, we had an understanding and accommodating editor. We were the eccentric Canadians who came from the wilderness with miles of film to assemble into a meaningful story. But the people we worked with seemed to appreciate our uniqueness and helped us make our life a success.

Being a country girl at heart, I loved to start the morning in our garden. The kids and I would venture out, tea in hand, barefoot, hair unbrushed, and wake up with the offerings of nature to greet us. A shy English robin, a slow-moving slug, a brightly coloured butterfly moving from flower to flower— these were our new friends. Behind the privacy of a high hedge, our dishevelled morning look didn't matter.

Our new home was a lovely, small, two-level building attached to a row of other homes. Ours was the first of about eight in the block, each with its own private garden. As we sat enjoying the morning air, taking in our new surroundings, the wind came up—a light breeze, but it had the strength to blow our door shut. Normally, a blown-shut door wouldn't be of much consequence, but today it changed everything. The wind was a catalyst.

When the door closed, it locked. We did not have a key outside with us and so we were in a bit of a fix. The phone was inside, so I couldn't call Jeff, and I would never walk into the BBC looking the way I did. Jeff wouldn't miss us for hours. It seemed we were stuck outside.

Then Chelsea remembered that the lady in cottage number 5 had a spare key. Chelsea had overheard the landlady tell Jeff the day before.

I didn't want to meet our new neighbours until I was more properly attired, so I decided to let the kids go and ask for the key. I would peek around the hedge and down the sidewalk, just in case this lovely old English lady wasn't as lovely as we hoped. So, off my children went on their own, and they were gone ever so long. *What could be happening? Should I go? No, wait a few more minutes. Go? No, wait.* And finally here they came, beaming as they walked towards me. The key didn't seem very important anymore. They had met this lady, Hazel!

"Mommy, do you know what she told us?"

Hazel had seen their auras, the beautiful, coloured light that shone around their bodies. She had described it to them and told them what it meant. I had heard of auras, but I wouldn't have expected them to come up in conversation while fetching a key. I thought the English were more conventional than this. And, much more amazingly, how did she see their auras? I'd never met someone who could do this.

Chelsea and Logan were so excited about this lady that they couldn't wait to go back and visit her.

"Could we go this afternoon? Mommy, you must come and visit. She has invited us any time."

I thought this was a nice gesture, but mostly I was relieved to get back into our home. We had so much to do, as I was sure Hazel did, so visiting her was not something I took seriously.

Chelsea and Logan took the key back the next day, and their enthusiasm for Hazel did not wane. Finally, a few days later, I agreed to go and meet the lady in number 5.

A beautiful wrought iron gate opened onto the path leading to her home. Hazel's lovely front garden was inviting and cheery, but as we knocked on the front door, I felt awkward and wondered what we could have to talk about.

When Hazel opened the door and I looked into her dancing eyes, I immediately felt comfortable. She ushered us into her sitting room as if we were special guests.

Hazel was petite, with large green eyes. It was hard to judge her age, but I would never have guessed she was eighty years old. Her shoulder-length hair had retained its youthful brunette colour. Her face was so gentle and kind, and I felt entirely at ease with her, as if I had known her forever.

Hazel was completely forthcoming, not at all reserved. She talked about Chelsea and Logan and wanted me to know what she felt and saw. She started by telling me what beautiful children they were, which every mother enjoys hearing. But then she went on to describe the light she saw around them. She said they were old souls. And then Hazel said that when she had seen Chelsea coming down the path, she had had a vision of her in a long green dress. It was an image of her from another lifetime, and it looked as though Chelsea had been royalty.

I had never decided whether I believed in reincarnation; really, I hadn't given it much thought. But as Hazel talked, I was absorbed by her every word and it all felt so natural, not unusual at all.

Hazel went on to say that she needed to be absolutely open and tell us the whole truth as she saw it, because she was getting older and didn't know how much longer she had to live. She did not mention that she was unwell, and because she had such a lively sparkle, I could not have guessed it. She wanted to share her experiences, wisdom, and understanding of life with us. Maybe she already knew what I did not: that it was time for me to hear what she had to say. Hazel was refreshingly honest and straightforward, and she could see that we were open and interested. She said that she couldn't afford to be self-conscious or to worry about what people thought about her. If she had something to offer, she would.

I loved Hazel almost from the moment I met her. I felt honoured to have the chance to spend time with her. There are few people whom I connect with, and very few whom I feel I can be my true self around. There is a superficiality around most relationships, and conversation tends to be guarded. But with Hazel, all the walls came down right from the start. I had no idea how this would translate in the future for me, but for now, Hazel added a new dimension to my already rich life.

Our film was coming together well, and our editor, Tim, was not only one of the best in the business but also a very good friend. The film was based on our family and the cougars that live in the mountains surrounding our home in British Columbia. Although the film starts on a sad note, with a cougar killing our dog Tess in our garden, it goes on to tell of our year getting to know and understand the cougars. Jeff had led the way, spending long days and nights searching with his camera for this elusive animal. On many wintry nights, Jeff trudged through the snow on his snowshoes to get into his blind, a small camouflaged tent where he filmed. He used an infrared light and camera to capture the mother cougar on film as she came in to feed on a dead deer.

On these dark nights, with Jeff miles away on the mountain, it was hard not to feel anxious and worry about him. The kids and I would wait by the two-way radio to hear his voice, broken with static, tell us he was safely in the blind. I kept the radio by my bed in case Jeff needed to call me. He often did not return until the early morning. When he did come back, we relived every moment of his night out.

The four of us are extremely close, and this film was the biggest thing in our lives that year. Chelsea, Logan, and I helped in every way we could, from collecting road-killed deer for the cougars to putting up filming blinds. On some days, we tracked cougars with Jeff. And on one outstanding day we got to meet a beautiful female as she watched us from a high tree branch. She lay gracefully posed, looking down on our excited family as we huddled in the snow, enjoying the magic of the moment.

The film highlights our home at Christmastime, and when I watch it, I am reminded of what a special and privileged life we lead. I am very grateful that we have been able to share these unforgettable experiences as a family. As we edited this film, it seemed appropriate that we, as a family, would all connect to Hazel and start this new journey of discovery together.

At this time in my life, things began moving with extreme swiftness in a new direction, in ways I couldn't comprehend. It was at times very difficult, and I'm not sure I could have handled the changes had it not been for Hazel's gentle guiding light.

The first sign of the changes was my waking in the middle of the night, in our little house down the lane from Hazel, and feeling restless to the point of being anxious and distraught. I got up and paced, and then I would lie down and try to calm myself. I felt some great pressure pushing on me. I couldn't understand what it was or where it was coming from. Night after night, I walked around, unable to sleep. Nothing in my life was unsettling. I had everything I had ever dreamed of. I loved being a mom and had wonderful children; I had a great relationship with Jeff, and a fulfilling career. There was nothing I was searching for. In fact, I felt as though I had life pretty much figured out. So where was this powerful, relentless pushing coming from? It was upsetting and exhausting, almost more than I could handle.

I sensed a message coming to me that I had to try harder, do more. It wasn't a voice; it was an intense feeling, a communication from something far greater than myself. Night after night, this feeling that I was to do something would descend on me, but I didn't know what I was to do or where this message was coming from. I was not a religious person and had never believed in the God that religious belief systems describe. I thought that subjects such as life after death would be addressed when I died; I didn't need answers now.

Now I felt I was being pressured to reach out for something more. Everyone would be sound asleep and the house would be dark and still. As I lay in bed, the uneasiness would come over me, as though someone was trying to talk to me. But I couldn't hear words or get a clear message, just this feeling that I was being told to do more, over and over. I remember calling out, "What do you want me to do? Do you want me to pray? I will pray if that's what you want, but what am I praying for? And to whom am I talking?" I did not get an answer.

A couple of days after this started, we found out from a neighbour that Hazel was in the hospital receiving treatment for cancer. I was shocked and distressed. How could such a strong and beautiful person have cancer? I felt very sorry for her, and although our friendship was just beginning, I already felt a deep emptiness at not seeing her. Her joyful energy was missing from our street and our lives. Anxious to know how she was doing, I could only wait for her to return. When she did come home, I could not believe how bad her condition was. Despite being larger than life, Hazel was very sick. The doctors had told her there was little they could do for her and that she had only a short time left.

So one night, as I lay in bed, unable to sleep and very much aware of this pressure to do something, I decided to take my thoughts to Hazel. Her treatment, I believe a type of chemotherapy, had burned her from the inside out. She had had a horrific reaction and came home from the hospital covered in burns, each one an inch or more across, now scabbing over. Although she never complained, it was clear just how uncomfortable she was.

I had no idea what I could do to help her, but I had heard of white light being used to heal or protect people. I thought it must be the purest form of light from the universe or a divine source. But it didn't really matter to me if I understood what it was or where it came from—it was the only thing I knew of that people did to heal others which used only the mind. My mind was all I had at two in the morning, and I desperately wanted to busy it with something. If I was feeling pressure to do more, then this is what I could do, even if I didn't really believe it would work.

I had no experience in what I was trying to do, and I didn't have much of a plan either. I imagined sending white light from our cottage, number 1, to Hazel's cottage, number 5, the light arcing up from me and down through Hazel's bedroom and into her head. I thought of it as meditation, something to focus my mind so I wouldn't feel the nagging pressure that kept me from sleeping.

The image came to me and it seemed a good one to go with. I pictured the light travelling through the top of Hazel's head, and my intention was to move it down through her neck, her arms, and her torso, down her legs, and out through her feet. Maybe, if such a thing as this light existed, it would bring her some peace or comfort in the night. But as I visualized the white light reaching the top of her chest, instead of it continuing in a straight line down her body, it burst into dozens of little balls of white light. Because this was not how I had planned for the light to move though Hazel's body, I started the process over again. Over and over, as the line of light moved into her body, it would burst into many balls that dissipated into her. I didn't understand what was happening, but I recognized that I had no control over it. I had initiated it, but then it moved beyond my comprehension and ability.

In the morning, our family routine carried on as normal: breakfast, school, editing. It seemed that my imagination had got away from me in the night. I thought that this week of crazy nights must be the result of stress I wasn't acknowledging. There was no need to discuss it with Jeff; I just hoped it would pass soon.

Hazel called later that morning, just as I was about to leave for work. She never phoned me, so it was a surprise.

"Thank you, Susan."

I didn't say anything, wondering what she meant.

"Thank you, Susan. All my scabs from my burns are completely gone. I'm healed. The doctor was in this morning to check on me and couldn't believe it. It wasn't possible for me to heal so quickly. They even stripped the bed and looked all through the sheets, but there wasn't a scab to be found."

When I went to see Hazel, her skin was clear. Hazel accepted the healing without question. I could admit something amazing had happened, but I didn't feel that I was at all responsible. Talking it over, Jeff and I could not begin to understand it. How was it physically possible? It was all so fantastic, but how else could we account for Hazel's changes, and how did she know what had taken place? Our choices were either to reject it, and put our heads in the sand because it was too much for us, or to accept it. We had only a few pieces of the puzzle, but from our extremely limited perspective we decided to accept what we had experienced.

I am so thankful Jeff was living this with me, because it was easy to see that our life view was changing. This was just the first of a series of events and teachings that would redirect the course of our future.

In the days that followed, my experiences were varied and many, and they came in quick succession. I think, because I have such a critical mind, if the experiences hadn't come quickly and kept my attention, doubt would have taken the upper hand and I would have dismissed the whole thing. I can never accept something just because someone tells me it's true. I like to analyze everything and figure out my own viewpoint. But every day seemed to bring something new.

At the BBC, my thoughts often turned to Hazel, and I would travel to her in my mind. I found it hard to focus on my work. Thank goodness, Jeff took up the slack. As I walked home one day, a voice told me there was more I could do to help Hazel. It was as if this relentless messenger found me very thick but thought that with repetition the message would eventually get through.

One afternoon, Chelsea and I went to visit Hazel. While we were sitting with her, I was overcome with an urge to do a healing. To my disbelief, I heard myself saying, "Hazel, would you like to come upstairs to your bed and I will do a healing for you?"

Chelsea's sweet face showed almost as much astonishment as I felt. My mind was leaping about, wondering what in the world I was talking about and, furthermore, what I was proposing to do. After all, I knew absolutely nothing about healing.

Hazel, knowing and calm, replied simply, "Yes, thank you, dear."

Another reason this was so startling is that I have always been squeamish around illness or physical injury. My older sisters became nurses, so when I was in high school I took work experience at our local hospital, thinking that maybe it was a field I'd be interested in as well. I lasted two days. I found it so upsetting that I had nightmares. I cannot stand blood or any bodily fluids or functions, and I have fainted at the sight of needles and scalpels. When my children were small, if they got a cut, I handed them a Band-Aid with my eyes closed. To this day I find hospitals and emergency rooms distressing. Furthermore, when one sister asked if I would study reiki with her and another asked if I would be interested in a healing touch course, although both seemed worthwhile, I couldn't summon up enthusiasm for either. Bodies in general are not my strong suit.

But having offered the healing, with neither the knowledge of how to do it nor the temperament for it, I was committed to try. Hazel had already started up the stairs, so Chelsea and I followed.

Hazel lay on her back on her bed. Seeing Chelsea's bewilderment, I suggested she rub Hazel's feet. Even at her young age, she was great at foot massages, so at least the situation wouldn't be a total loss. I put my hands on Hazel—I can't remember where. My mind was blank. Almost immediately, my right hand started to move, my left hand staying still. My right hand moved around, stopping in places to pat or circle. I was not consciously controlling it; my hand seemed to move on its own. Although the movement wasn't tiring, the energy coming into me started to overwhelm me. There came a point when I stopped my right hand because I was completely overcome. I started to cry. I believe now that the crying was an energy release, but at the time I felt embarrassed and confused.

Hazel took it all in stride. She told me my hand had worked in all the places she had pain and that now the pain had eased. She said it was natural to cry and that I shouldn't be concerned about it.

Afterwards, as we sat in her sitting room, she began to tell Chelsea and me about her early life in India.

Hazel was English, but she had been born in India and was raised there until she went to boarding school overseas.

She returned after graduation to her parents' home in Chennai (Madras), in southern India. When Hazel was a child, her mother worked with Indian healers, and Hazel would help by carrying a dish of water so the healers could wash their hands and arms after each healing; they were rinsing off the energy from the patient, not washing away germs.

In her young adult life, Hazel married a man who was a very high-ranking superintendent of India's railway lines, which allowed Hazel to travel all over the country. She remained interested in healers and the spiritual aspects of life, and as she travelled around, she met Indians who were practising healing and spiritual living. She told us of an Indian man who sat under a tree and did healings on people who came to him. It seemed that energy healing was quite common and accepted in India.

Hazel had gained much experience over the years and was very gifted herself with psychic and mediumistic skills. At times, she was able to see and communicate with spirits. She also had premonitions and dreams of future events. One night, she and her husband were asleep on a train. Hazel suddenly woke him to tell him she had dreamed that a train bridge ahead, which spanned a large ravine, had been burned out. Thankfully, her husband believed her, respecting her abilities, and had the train stopped. Some men who worked on the train walked ahead, and sure enough, the bridge had been burned out.

Hazel told us many such stories during our visits. What beautiful timing it was that she had come into my life now. For the first time, I felt entirely open to the possibilities, and I greatly needed Hazel by my side to explain the many experiences I was having and keep me grounded.

It seems as though, during this time in England, I was being shown many different types of spiritual or energetic situations. One day Hazel came over to have dinner with us. We had asked her to come early because we never could have enough time with her. She and Chelsea were in our sitting room, having their own special time together, looking at a collection of small perfume bottles that Chelsea had just bought at a local shop. All the bottles were different shapes and each perfume had a special name. Jeff was still at work, and Logan, who had been feeling sick, was asleep in our bedroom. I had to pop out to the store to get some ingredients for dinner. I asked Chelsea to stay out of the bedroom because it was important that Logan sleep.

As I came through our garden gate on my return home, I glanced up at the window of our second-floor bedroom. I was disappointed to see someone in the room going through the top drawer of my dresser. In the shadows cast by the late afternoon light, I couldn't see who it was but assumed it must be Chelsea. This, I thought, would surely wake Logan.

But when I went inside, Hazel and Chelsea were sitting on the sofa exactly where I had left them. I told them what I'd seen. Could it be an intruder trying to steal something? Up the stairs I went, my protective instincts for Logan far outweighing my fear for myself. But Logan was sleeping soundly, and there was no one to be found anywhere upstairs. Nevertheless, I had absolutely no doubt that I had seen a person standing by my dresser, going through the top drawer.

Hazel explained that it could have been the spiritual energy of someone who had once lived in the house. I had never seen a person in spirit before, and actually seeing one that looked like a person in physical form was even more amazing. It seemed I was in the perfect state of openness to witness this new dimension. I liked the thought of people living on in spiritual energy, and didn't find it scary in the least. This experience excited me, and having Hazel there to explain it made it feel quite natural. There was no doubt that my world view was changing quickly.

After dinner, while Jeff and Chelsea did the washing-up in the kitchen and Hazel and I sat at the table, I had a strong impulse to put my hands on her head. Hazel was keen for me to try, even though I didn't know what I would do. I stood behind her and placed my hands just above her ears. I began to feel energy moving through, up, and around the top of her head in a circle. My hands moved faster and faster, from her ears up to the top of her head and back down. The energy was intense. It continued for about ten minutes. My eyes were closed, but my eyelids started to flutter with what felt like excess energy. It increased until I felt as if I was going to levitate. At this point I became aware of this strong energy, and I made my hands stop. I was overwhelmed and a little frightened. It seemed as though I was losing control of my body.

Hazel said that she had felt the energy moving around and through her head, and it had felt good to her. Later, she told me that she stopped taking morphine because her pain was gone. Months later the pain did come back, but for a time the healing work I had done seemed to help her.

A couple of days later, I had another unusual experience. While out shopping, I felt a strong urge to buy Hazel a present. It was like a conversation in my mind. I was told to go into a bookstore and buy a book for Hazel. My rational mind answered that I really didn't know what kind of book Hazel would want, or if she would even want one at all. Finally, persuaded to go into the bookstore, I was pulled to a section that had John Edward's book about his life as a medium. I had never heard of John Edward; although he is famous, his experience was not a topic I knew anything about. Before I met Hazel, I had never even heard the word "medium," but I had learned from her that a medium is the communicator between a person in Spirit energy and a person in physical form. I didn't feel comfortable buying Hazel this book; she wasn't well and it might seem that I was implying she would die soon and therefore needed to read about mediums. But the persuasive voice in my mind was quite keen on it. Finally, thinking I had no cash and not wanting to use my credit card for a purchase of only ten pounds, I made a deal with the voice: if I could find the money in my purse, I would buy the book, otherwise I would forget about it. I was certain I didn't have any cash and this looked like an easy way out.

This sounds silly, I'm sure—having a discussion with a voice in my head about whether or not to buy a book—but I'm a strong-minded person and was not used to having Spirit tell me what to do. I'm sure most people have experienced a strong impulse inside, pushing them to do a certain thing. So often I've heard people say, "If only I had listened to that little voice in my head" or, as my grandmother would say, "A little bird told me." This was similar, but the conversation went on and on. It happens to me regularly now, and I know I'm communicating with someone in the spirit world, maybe one of my guides or a loved one who has passed over.

I looked in my purse and wallet: no money, as I had expected. Then the back pocket of my purse opened slightly, revealing a ten-pound note inside. I couldn't believe it—I never put money in that pocket. That ten-pound note seemed to confirm that I really was meant to buy the book. So I did, and when I gave it to Hazel, she couldn't have been more pleased. Months before, she'd been clearing out her things and had given away most of her books, but now she really missed them. She had enjoyed reading books written by mediums, and she felt this book would be comforting at this time in her life. The book was so right for Hazel that I believe I was guided to buy it for her, and the voice was no doubt someone in the spirit world who knew her. Whoever it was, I'm sure they felt I was incredibly difficult to work with; I questioned the messages I was receiving every step of the way.

Almost every day, I experienced something of a spiritual nature, and it was convincing me that there is a lot more to our lives than what we see in the physical. I needed years with Hazel, not months, both as a friend and as a guide. She was so humble and yet incredibly wise. I could not imagine going back to Canada and leaving her behind. But the day arrived when our film was complete and we were packing to go. Saying goodbye to Hazel, hugging her for the last time, was one of the hardest things I have ever done. I knew I would not see her again. I desperately wanted her in my day-to-day life, but it was not possible.

When I got home, I phoned Hazel almost every day and we exchanged many letters in what would be the last few months of her life. Because we always ended our calls and letters with our love, admiration, and appreciation for each other, Hazel would always say "Ping-Pong": just like the ball in a Ping-Pong game, all of the goodness is coming right back to you. They were such fun and loving words.

I wanted to travel to England to see Hazel, but she did not want Chelsea and Logan to see her when she was so sick and I didn't want to travel so far from my children, so I had to make the difficult decision never to see her again. Hazel told me that when she died, she would use roses as a symbol to let me know she was there in spirit.

On the day Hazel passed, I had taken Chelsea to a singing lesson in a nearby town. I went for a walk as I waited, and found the loveliest rose garden in someone's backyard, with dozens of rose bushes in every colour. As I admired their beauty, a feeling came over me that Hazel had died. I knew she was gone. I think she led me to the garden and then quietly gave me the news.

I was doing a healing on my mom recently when I felt Hazel near me. I spoke to her in my mind, and she reassured me that my mom would be all right. As I continued working, my mom said that she could see the most beautiful rose in front of her, a wild rose of pristine pink. She was moved because it was so detailed and unexpected. I was extremely pleased, but not all that surprised—as always, Hazel brings forth so much love, generosity, and kindness.

Hazel, Ping-Pong.

A GOLD RIBBON

HAD COME HOME from England with extreme sadness, for I knew I would never see Hazel again. How could someone you want and need so badly be with you for such a brief time?

I knew I must continue along the path Hazel had started me on, but I was taking baby steps. Would the healing energy I had experienced in England work the same way in Canada, or was it connected only to Hazel? I wanted to try it on someone to see if my hands would still move, but I was unsure. Working with Hazel had felt safe; it all seemed so natural to her. I didn't have anyone in Canada who felt like a teacher or a guide. I was coming home a different person and I did not know where to turn. Strange and amazing energy had come out of my hands, but I didn't understand how it worked or where it came from.

Because I had no conscious understanding of what was happening, I did not want to take a course in healing. I didn't want to let an intellectual process get in the way of what was happening naturally. I had some confidence in the energy, but I had virtually no confidence in myself. The healing happened in spite of me, and I did not want to intellectualize it. I respected that what was happening far surpassed the human mind.

But I had so much to learn about where this path would take me. I could accept not understanding the healing energy, but I wanted to know what it meant to me and how I was to live my life from now on. Hazel had talked about mediums. Maybe a medium could help me understand my life direction a little better. When I got home, the one thing I felt certain of was that I wanted to have a reading with a medium.

My sister Leanne knew about a psychic fair taking place in a nearby town, so we decided to see what it was all about. Jeff left us there before going off to do some business and we agreed to meet in the early afternoon.

As Leanne and I entered the hall, I was amazed at all the booths set up in the big open room. We had to pick someone we would like to see and sign up at the front desk. Some people were dressed in New Age clothing, and many of the tables were decorated with candles, crystals, cloth, and pictures. I felt out of place and not really comfortable with anyone I could see.

Leanne and I split up to explore the hall. I finally decided on a man I would ask for a reading. He had a table by the window. His location on the edge of all this strange business made him seem a little less daunting. We were not far into the reading when he began to cry. He said my energy was quite intense and overwhelming. I have no memory of the messages he told me.

I then went to a flamboyant woman dressed in bright colours and long scarves. Her table was very busy and highly decorated. I remember little of what she said, except that one day I would do some writing—something I had never thought of doing—and that I would have different guides helping me. One would be Kuan Yin. I had no idea who Kuan Yin was, and I completely forgot about this until years later.

By the time I met up with Leanne, I was feeling a little underwhelmed. I don't know what I had expected, but I just felt so out of place there. I couldn't relate to most of these people, and I was disappointed. Leanne, though, had had an incredible reading with a medium. She said there was no elaborate set-up; it was simple but amazing. She suggested I sign up right away because she thought this medium would be booked up soon. There was just one opening left at the end of the day, so I booked it for Jeff and myself.

Jeff and I sat down opposite the medium at a little round wooden table. She was a young woman with short, fine light-brown hair, a roundish face, and cheerful eyes behind wire-rimmed glasses. She introduced herself as Dana. Straightforward in her manner, she came across as the girl next door, not at all mysterious. I instantly felt very comfortable. She was just the person I had hoped to meet, a talented medium, and I wished to know her better. I was sure Hazel would have liked her. The reading wasn't taped, but a few things she said I have never forgotten.

First, she said that Jeff and I were very connected and had an important purpose together in this lifetime. She saw a gold ribbon wrapped around us. She asked if I was a doctor or in the medical field. I was pleased, because I felt she was seeing the healing energy. She went on to describe our home and its surroundings. She saw our log home in the trees on the side of a mountain. She also saw a fire burning in the fireplace in the living room and a dog lying in front of it.

Then she connected to the spirit of Tess, our beloved German shepherd, whom we had lost a few years before. She described her perfectly and said she was always around us, still protecting us. Tess had been a best friend to me, my constant companion, and had helped me get through early motherhood. I had relied on her when I was alone with my babies in remote filming locations. She was a very wise being and brought me great comfort, so I was thrilled to have her come through to us.

But then Dana said that the one thing Tess was sad about was that she had never been able to have her own babies, that she had lost them. I was shocked. Nobody knew.

When Tess was quite young, still a pup really, and not yet spayed, she got pregnant. She had jumped out of the back of our truck through the canopy window while we were having dinner at a roadside pub. When I came out to the truck, she was in the company of a male dog. I wasn't sure they had had a relationship, but I thought it was likely.

I took Tess to the vet to be spayed. She was much too young to have puppies. When I left her at the vet, I didn't know if she was pregnant or not. When I picked her up, the vet told me there were nine embryos. It was a difficult and horrible situation, but the vet felt we had chosen well: Tess was very young to be a mother and there were too many unwanted dogs in the world. The painful experience was over and I never wanted to go there in my mind again. Now, years after her death, Tess was telling me it was her one sorrow. I cannot tell you what an enormous impact this had on me.

Jeff and I left the reading in utter amazement. The overall feeling we had was one of empowerment. We felt close to each other and inspired to do our very best. There was so much more to our existence than we had realized, so many more resources for us to call upon to find our way, such a broad foundation for us to work from, so much more meaning to our lives. Before, I had never cared whether people did or didn't carry on in another life after they died—I could not see that it had any significance to my life. The thought of my existence coming to a complete end did not bother me at all. In fact, it made everything much simpler, and I could feel much less responsible. But now I was beginning to understand that if our lives continue instead of ending at the time of our physical death, then how we live and the choices we make become very important. The realization that our life energy continues was a total game changer. The person we choose to be at this deeper level, our relationship to other people, to animals, and to the Earth—they all matter, because we will have to come to terms with the consequences of our actions and emotional choices. But with this new-found responsibility also came the understanding that we are not alone, that we always have help in our life's journey. And all the effort we put into living a good life makes a much greater difference than we might imagine.

When the layers of life are so intertwined and interconnected, each choice creating a series of consequences, the meaning of these choices becomes profound. We were beginning to realize the significance of our lives: that they are not simply a series of unrelated events without a meaningful outcome, but rather a very purposeful journey.

LIVING WITH BEARS

MY JOURNEY WITH Jeff to this point had been about making films and living in the wild. We understood on a deep level our connection to animals and nature. Then we had a transformative experience, beyond anything we could have imagined, when we spent two years living on a remote coastal island of British Columbia.

We went to the island to make a film about the white Kermode bears, or spirit bears as they are now known. They belong to the black bear species but have a white coat. At the time we went to film, most people hadn't heard of these incredible white bears because they are found in only a very small area of BC. We thought they were magical. We also learned that their island was about to be logged and they weren't protected from hunting. We hoped that our film would let people see the great beauty of the island and the uniqueness of the spirit bears, and motivate them to help protect the bears.

It would be a huge and exciting project. Jeff and I decided to move to the island with Chelsea, who was only six months old. The island was otherwise uninhabited and was very far off the beaten path, so it would be challenging. Knowing we would need help, we asked our good friend Charlie Russell to come and live and work with us.

We had originally got to know Charlie when we wanted his help filming grizzlies. We were making a film for the CBC to bring awareness of the critical importance of saving the grizzlies' diminishing habitat. At that time we didn't know Charlie, but we knew a lot about his family. His grandfather, Bert Riggall, was a well-known Canadian photographer and naturalist. His father, Andy Russell, was famous for the books he wrote about animals and the wilderness. He was also renowned for making the first grizzly bear film with his sons, Charlie and Dick. When I was a little girl, about five years old, my mom and dad took our family to an evening talk Andy was giving at our local school, as he travelled through the country showing his film. My mom took me in my pyjamas, because she knew I would be asleep before we got home that night. Twenty-five years later, Andy fondly told me the story of seeing a little girl in the front row at one of his talks in her PJs. He was surprised when I told him it was me. Andy's talk and film had always stood out in my mind, I think because it was such a big deal for our family to meet someone as famous as Andy and his sons.

When we started filming grizzlies, a biologist recommended that we ask Charlie Russell to work with us. He had more experience and knowledge of bears than anyone else. When Jeff decided to call him at his home in Waterton, Alberta, I was shocked. I couldn't imagine anyone of Charlie's calibre having the time to help two unknown filmmakers. Jeff and I were just twenty-six at the time, and this was only our second film. To my amazement, Charlie said he would like to come and help. And as they say, the rest is history. The white bear film followed our grizzly film.

Charlie had grown up in the wilderness with his family, so he had a lot of expertise setting up detailed bush camps. Jeff and Charlie left in the spring of 1992 to set up an extensive camp that would be our home for the next two years. There were five canvas wall tents in total. Three were sleep tents, all with plywood floors, beds, and wood stoves—one for Jeff, Chelsea, and me, one for Charlie, and one for guests. There was a cook tent with a dining table, a wood stove, a propane cooking stove and propane fridge, and a sink with running water. And there was a storage tent for camera gear and food. We also had a shower house and toilet.

I arrived a few weeks later with Chelsea. The trip to the island included a very long drive, a ferry, a float plane, and ended with Jeff picking me up at a tiny coastal village with our twenty-foot aluminum boat. It was a foggy day and the water was choppy. I put lifejackets on Chelsea and myself, and we sat on the floor of the boat to get out of the wind. Jeff and I knew little about living on the ocean, and as we pounded up and down over the waves on our way to our new home, the magnitude of what we had embarked on really started to sink in.

Our life on the island was busy. Jeff and Charlie went out filming each day. Chelsea and I went out with the guys some days, but otherwise we stayed in camp. Camp life for me entailed entertaining Chelsea, cooking meals, baking bread, and doing laundry by hand. I was naive enough to have brought only cloth diapers for Chelsea. They were mostly fine, but trying to keep up with drying them in the tents when it would sometimes rain for ten days straight was challenging. I also tried planting a little vegetable garden, but the sandy soil and abundant rain prevented much success. Thankfully, we had a marine band two-way radio, and about once a month we would send messages out and order a few supplies to be brought in by float plane or boat. We were known on the coast as Camp Chelsea.

Beyond our camp were steep mountains covered with dense trees and bush. Mountain creeks rushed down to the ocean. Their rocky edges were our corridors for hiking into the heart of the island. I had a sturdy backpack for carrying Chelsea. She loved the outdoors and she loved seeing animals. As long as she was on my back and we were moving, she was happy.

We had come to the island to film bears, especially white bears, but we also filmed wolves, eagles, whales, otters, and any other animals that we met. Filming with the bears really got started in the late summer, when the salmon arrived to spawn in the creeks. The bears emerged from the thick vegetation of the forests to the pools of water where they could catch fish. The pools gave us a place to go where we were quite certain to find bears.

The first time we saw a white bear on the creek, we were thrilled beyond belief. We had gone months on the island and hadn't seen one, and they had begun to seem like mythical creatures. When the spirit bear appeared, it was almost surreal. Its white fur radiated like a beacon of light. I felt I needed to pinch myself to see if the moment was real. We were anxious we might never see one again, because being with a spirit bear seemed too good to be true.

But we did see the spirit bear again, and others, as well as lots of black bears. In the months that followed, our life with the bears was up close and personal. They had no fear of us. They didn't have any experience with humans, and had no preconceived ideas of how we would behave. The relationship we offered them formed their opinion of us. We offered them love, kindness, respect, and admiration. They returned with gentleness, respect, and friendship. It was so real and honest. Living in such untouched wilderness with animals who totally accepted us into their lives felt sacred. It was a privilege, and it appeared to us that we were living as we are meant to, in peace and harmony.

The bears could sense our emotions, and I think they could see our energy. They could tell we meant them no harm. They would look at us and then go about fishing, treating us as we were, just other animals on the creek. Experiencing a relationship with wild animals where we are all one and the same made me understand our human place on the Earth in a way I had never grasped before. Being so completely connected to the truth and beauty of the natural world created an effortless link to my soul. I felt I knew myself better than I ever had.

Charlie was what I can best describe as a "bear interpreter," because he was so good at understanding what bears are feeling and what they are trying to tell people when they have interactions with them. He had accumulated this insight through dedicating most of his life to working and living with bears. He was not encumbered by what other people thought, and formed his own opinions based on what he saw and experienced. Over a lifetime, he had observed that bears are not what most of society thinks they are. His experiences around bears showed him an animal that is tolerant and accepting of people. He felt it was our fear of bears that got in the way of our understanding them. Through most of human history, bears have been hunted, persecuted, or driven to extinction in many places where they lived. Bears learned to be afraid of humans, and most people feel it's a good thing if a bear runs away in fear. Charlie didn't agree. He was so soft-spoken and gentle with them. He wanted people to understand that a fearful bear is more likely to become dangerous. If a bear has had a negative experience with people, it might react with aggression to protect itself, the same way we might lash out if pushed and harassed repeatedly. In my opinion, he was the best in the world at really understanding the true character of bears.

From the day I met Charlie, I had an unusual connection to him. I felt as though I had always known him; he felt like a brother to me, and still does. Jeff, Charlie, and I also became very close because of our shared love of bears and our deep desire to protect them and teach people how to understand their true nature.

A young spirit bear became not only the star of our film but also a good friend to all of us. He was about three or four years old and no longer with his mother. In the bear world, he did not have much seniority. On the creeks, it's the biggest, oldest bears that get to fish in the best places, and our spirit bear would often be chased off by the dominant bears. He learned, however, that if he fished by us, the other bears would leave him alone. So he would often stay only a few feet from us, sometimes smelling the camera lens to see what Jeff was doing.

But it wasn't just about his access to fishing spots. He completely trusted Jeff and Charlie as they entered into his world to record the details of his life. Sometimes, when they were away from the creek with him, he would want to play with them, the way a dog likes to play. He would tussle with the end of a stick that one of the guys would be holding.

He would race around, running back and forth, almost as if he was playing tag with them. This particular bear went beyond being fearless of Jeff and Charlie; he made a special bond with them. They could follow him up into the forest, where he would bed down in the moss for an afternoon nap. They would sit quietly with him, watching this exquisite bear sleeping as the afternoon sunlight filtered through the branches of the trees and across his white fur. Jeff and Charlie appreciated the fact that this bear could sleep, in total peace, while they were there.

Our time on the island instilled in Charlie a desire to understand what would be possible with grizzly bears if he could find a place where they lived unencumbered by fear of humans. He wanted to have relationships with them based on respect and love, and come to know the true nature of these magnificent animals. This desire eventually took him to the wilds of the Kamchatka Peninsula in Russia.

All the animals on the island trusted us and accepted us into their home. One day, while Chelsea and I were alone at camp, I took her down to the beach. I had a little thirty-six-inch child's swimming pool for Chelsea to sit and play in; it kept her away from pebbles that she would want to put into her mouth. As we sat in the sunshine, I looked over and saw a black bear. She was sitting in a small pool of water amongst the rocks in the creek that flowed down from the mountain by our camp. She was relaxing and cooling off from the afternoon sun. I thought how incredibly beautiful it was that we could be there together, just enjoying the day.

For Chelsea, I think starting life with such a close connection to the natural world was one of the greatest gifts we could have given her. She was so at ease with the bears and wolves, growing up with them as her neighbours. One evening I stood on the shore below our camp, holding Chelsea over my shoulder, enjoying the view down the inlet. She was looking off in the opposite direction. In her little voice, she said, "Woff." Surprised to hear her speaking, I asked her what she was saying. She repeated herself, saying "woff" a bit more strongly. I wasn't quite sure if she was actually saying a word, and turned to look in her direction. There, farther along the shoreline, standing on the rocks and looking out to sea, was a majestic black wolf. Wow. A lifetime memory of Chelsea's first word etched in my mind.

We created two films: *Islands of the Ghost Bear*, a natural history film, and *Trusting Bears*, a thirty-minute documentary the BBC produced about us living on the island with the bears. But by far the greatest gift Jeff and I received from living on the island was the sensation of pureness of being, something we rarely get to experience in the human world. It opened our consciousness to another level. Looking back, I think it was this experience that opened our minds to possibilities in life far beyond what we could have imagined. It made seemingly hidden worlds more tangible.

GUIDES

IT WAS VERY exciting to have met Dana. She had taken us into another world we hadn't experienced before. And because she was a gifted psychic medium, we were able to have a phenomenal introduction to this new way of seeing.

Before Jeff and I left the fair, we made an appointment to bring Chelsea and Logan to Dana's home a couple of weeks later for a family reading. We were so thrilled by this new way of seeing that we wanted the kids to experience it as well, and doing so kept us united as a family.

The four of us sat together on Dana's sofa, listening intently as she brought through the Spirit energy surrounding each of us, from our animal guides to our spirit guides. She said that animal guides feature in many cultures around the world, especially those that honour and respect nature. They offer spiritual guidance by drawing our attention to the symbolism they represent. Each animal has its own meaning or interpretation. She said different animal guides may show up at different times in our lives, but most people have one main animal guide that is with them throughout their life. Dana told us that she saw a grizzly bear with Jeff and a white tiger with me.

Dana said that in addition to animal guides, we also have spirit guides. Their role is to guide or observe us on our spiritual journey as humans, and, like animal guides, they change throughout our lives. Spirit guides can introduce other guides, who represent new areas where we need help solving problems. There are different types of spirit guides, and they can be male or female. Their presence is symbolic of what they are helping us with or teaching us on our path. For example, your spirit guide might be a warrior or a shaman, and this could mean specific things based on what you are encountering or going through at the time. If you do energy or healing work, you may have older guides or master guides who work with more than one person. Ancestral guides are loved ones who have advanced in the spirit world and are now filling the role of guardians or helpers from the spirit world. You share these master guides with other people, and their primary goal is to help all of humanity.

None of this information seemed strange or scary. On the contrary, it felt quite normal, light, and happy. It brought death and Spirit into our lives in a positive way. These are often taboo subjects in our society, but they're actually natural aspects of our lives.

Dana invited us to a two-day course in psychic development at her home. I decided to go with Chelsea, Leanne, and another friend. Dana lived a few hours' drive away and we made the trip with great anticipation. She had been so accurate and informative in our readings that I couldn't wait to have more time with her.

We spent the first day meditating and doing psychic exercises, such as trying to perceive what was in envelopes and picking up the energy of people in old photographs. I wasn't particularly good at any of the activities, and I have a tendency to get a little restless in classroom situations. My mind wandered and I found myself examining the overall situation of the class. Dana had another woman working with her, and I was struck by how their energies didn't go well together. This lack of connection became forefront in my mind.

On the morning of the second day, I tried my own psychic exercise to see if I could send Dana a message telepathically. I thought that if I kept repeating something over and over in my mind, and sending it to Dana, if we were connected, she would pick it up.

At the mid-morning break, Dana said that we would pair up and do small readings with each other. She told everyone to find a partner and then said quite bluntly, "Sue will be my partner. Come to the kitchen."

Once we were in the kitchen, Dana gave me a very no-nonsense look that made me feel like a naughty schoolchild.

"Okay," she said, "what are you trying to tell me? I could hear you all morning. What is it?"

I told her I didn't think she and the other gal were working well together. Dana was real and gifted, but the other person did not inspire confidence and did not help Dana in her teaching. I felt that she would turn off clients, and that it was in Dana's best interest to work without her. Dana agreed and said she didn't really feel at ease with her. The fact that I could communicate with Dana telepathically said more about Dana than about me, but we obviously had a connection.

This was the beginning of a friendship that was not only fun and exciting, but also timely and meaningful. It allowed me to experience many new realms in the psychic and mediumistic world. The wish I had made at the fair, to get to know Dana better, had been answered.

Dana and I were different in some ways, but we shared a sense of humour and a love of Spirit energy. Dana, although she was a brilliant medium, never entertained a big ego. She was down-to-earth, open, and willing to work with me.

Dana often came to stay at our house. She loved the country setting and the chance to recharge her batteries from her continuous schedule of readings. Because she did not have children of her own, she liked to partake in our family life.

One day, while we were sitting by the pond in our garden, Dana said, "Did you used to have a white duck?"

"Yes," I replied, "many years ago. She was the first duck we ever had. She was killed by an owl."

"Well, she's wandering around in the grass right now." Dana could see the spirit form of our duck in her mind's eye, as if she were watching a movie clip.

I loved the spontaneity of these experiences and how the spirit world blended with our physical world. Dana was always telling me little details and they were always correct. I felt it was an amazing gift to see spirit beings appear through the energy of our physical plane. Nothing about it scared me. I loved every moment that Dana shared her images with me.

The lighter and happier you are, the easier it is for Spirit to communicate, because the frequency of your energy is higher and therefore closer to the frequency of Spirit. Excited and fascinated, I couldn't understand why most people didn't want to talk about this. But from the very beginning, it felt like something you did not bring up in conversation because it made so many people uncomfortable.

With Dana, I was free to be as open as I wanted—nothing was too weird or off the table. She offered a safe place for me to discover and learn about the world of Spirit energy, and she loved to share information and insights.

Over the years, Dana did many readings for Jeff and me, sometimes helping us with difficult decisions related to our wildlife films. For one project, Jeff had gone to Russia with Charlie to film grizzly bears. Charlie had been living with grizzlies in the wilderness of Kamchatka, in the far east of Russia, for ten years. One of the most important elements of the story was supposed to be filming four two-year-old bears coming out of their den. Charlie had raised these bears from when they were very young cubs, after their mother was killed by poachers. But due to complications getting into Russia, when Jeff and Charlie finally arrived at the den site out in the wilderness, the bears had already left. It was a devastating blow to our film and to Charlie, who was anxious to reconnect with his bear family. Jeff and Charlie searched everywhere for the young bears, but couldn't find them.

Searching on foot in the Russian wilderness is no easy feat. Jeff, desperate, called home on a satellite phone. I immediately contacted Dana for an emergency reading. She said she could clearly see two young bears roaming across the land, but there was no sign of the other two. She said these two who were roaming were doing fine, and she felt they were near Charlie's cabin.

Weeks passed and spring rolled into summer, but there was still no sign of the bears. Then one morning two handsome, healthy bears showed up at Charlie's door. It took a few moments for Charlie to recognize them, for they had grown so much since he had seen them ten months earlier.

They were no longer the small cubs Charlie had left behind last fall. But they were very keen to see him again. They had been out to experience the world, but were now happy to be home. They became two of the most beloved film stars we ever had.

While Charlie and Jeff were in Russia, I had my clearest visitation so far from someone in spirit. It was Charlie's dad. He came to me before I heard that he had passed. I was completely relaxed, having an afternoon bubble bath, when suddenly, standing by the end of the tub, there was Andy. I hadn't known him well, but years before, when Chelsea was only two, Jeff, Chelsea, and I had spent a memorable Easter weekend with Andy and Charlie. I felt that Andy and I had connected in some way. He was an old man then, so while Charlie and Jeff spent long days finishing the building of Charlie's ultralight airplane, Andy, Chelsea, and I hung out together in their mountain home. Andy had said that if I did the cooking, he would buy everything we needed for a big family Easter dinner, so the three of us drove into town, about a forty-minute drive, and bought everything for a feast. When we got back, I spent hours in the kitchen cooking, while Chelsea sat on Andy's knee and talked away to him. She called him Annie, as she couldn't quite say his name, and that made him smile.

Andy was very charismatic. I think that, because he had such a big personality, it was easier for him to bring his energy through to me. So there I was, soaking in the bubbles, when I saw him. I would have felt embarrassed if he had been there in his physical body, but he was in spirit. He had been quite sick in a retirement home. Now Andy spoke of how happy he was to be free of his tired, unwell body. He came through so clearly that his joyful energy became part of me, and I felt incredibly uplifted and happy. So even though he had died, we were both in a cheerful mood because he was in a good place now.

I think he came to let me know he was helping Charlie and Jeff in Russia as they tried to find the grizzlies. Like Charlie, he had spent his life with bears, and he was ready to get out of bed and back into the field. He visited me about four times over the next couple of months, and I was always glad to see him. He was a liaison between the guys in Russia and me. I felt that he was there for all of us.

One day, when Dana visited me, Andy came as well. She did not know him at all, had never seen a picture of him, but described a man in my kitchen wearing a large Stetson hat and a fringed leather jacket. That was Andy's signature outfit. I was so happy that she had a chance to meet him, and once again it was helpful that Dana, an experienced medium, could confirm that I was receiving information from Spirit.

I always needed reassurance that the healing was part of who I am. It was such a foreign way of being that I thought I must be fooling myself. I had yet to meet or read about anyone who had the same experience of healing as I did, without any conscious input or awareness of what was going on, so I was constantly questioning myself. I also kept it mostly a secret, only discussing it with some family members and close friends. I worried about people finding out and judging me, and about embarrassing my family. Living in a small town, I wanted to maintain the persona of a "normal" woman. But with Dana, who herself lived on the edge of typical social behaviour, I felt comfortable and free both to experiment with the healing and to express my feelings.

On one of Dana's visits, she told me she was having trouble with her sciatic nerve and asked if I would work on her back. I was always excited to explore the possibilities for healing and I wanted to work on as many different situations as possible. Dana lay on her stomach on what I call my healing table—it's a massage table but works well for this type of healing—and I put my hands on her back. When I start a healing, I move my right hand over the person, just above the skin. When it reaches an area that needs working on, my hand starts to vibrate and then moves in patterns, alternating between patting, making circles, and other types of movements. If I know the person has a particular problem, I go to that area and wait for my hand to start working. I have no conscious awareness of what my hand is doing or why. I must leave my intellect out of it; often my mind is off somewhere totally unrelated, maybe thinking about what to make for dinner or what flowers to put in my planters. From time to time I check in with my hand to see what it's doing and how my patient seems to be. Usually the patient is in a state of deep relaxation or has gone to sleep. When a healing is finished, my hand simply quits moving.

My hand moved across Dana's shoulder and down her arm. The healing movements went directly to her elbow and down to her wrist. My medical knowledge may be very limited, but I knew this was not the area of her sciatic nerve. I also knew it was not my place to judge or get involved with this healing, so I took my mind elsewhere and let my hand continue its work. When it stopped, I was curious as to what Dana would say and confused about why I hadn't worked on her back.

After the healing session, Dana straightened up and gave me a knowing smile. She said she had carpal tunnel syndrome. She hadn't told me before because she thought the condition couldn't be healed with energy. The carpal tunnel was so bad that she was no longer able to write or work on her computer. She had started writing a book but was afraid she could not continue without having an operation to correct the problem. This healing turned out to be an instant fix. Dana never again had trouble with her wrist, and today she writes on a steady basis.

Healings like this thrilled me, confused me, and left me wondering what it was all about. I searched for answers in my mind and in books about other healers. I read about a man in England who would go into a trance and then a spirit would move into his energy field and do the healing. I did not feel this was what was happening with me, but I didn't know what *was* happening.

My hand moved of its own accord, without my conscious control. In almost every healing, the movement was something I couldn't have imagined before I began, so it seemed I couldn't be creating this ability with my own thoughts. And it didn't always move or vibrate. Sometimes I would put my hand on someone and nothing would happen. I don't know why this was, but it meant there was no way to go ahead with the healing.

I was a person who liked to plan and be organized. Jeff and I had mapped out our lives quite carefully—what films we would make, when we would have children, who would work with us. I liked to have a one-year plan, a three-year plan, and a five-year plan. Working freelance brought uncertainty, but I loved the freedom, and finding our own work made us feel that we were in control of our lives. With the healings, I had to give up all control. I didn't know what the energy was or where it came from. I didn't know if or when it would be successful. I didn't know if my hands would move on someone, or how they would move. The movement could be very slow or so fast I wondered how I could keep up. I couldn't set up a session with someone and say I'd work on them for half an hour, because it could be over in fifteen minutes or go on for forty.

Lack of control is completely different from free choice. I always have free choice to do the healings or not. I am drawn to do them, and while I can refuse, doing so would be hard on me. Once the message starts to come through that I should do a healing for someone, there is no peace for me until I commit myself to the person by offering the healing. Once I am in, I give up control over the plan of action. It is exciting, because each healing is a unique journey and I never know what will be uncovered or what my patient and I will experience. At the same time, not knowing what will happen can be unnerving. All I can do is offer my assistance, let go, and see what happens.

ENERGY

THE FIRST PERSON I worked on when I came home from England was my sister Leanne. I had told her about my amazing experiences with Hazel and she was hopeful I could help her. She was having a lot of back pain and could barely walk. As I put my hands on her back, I thought, *Will this work in Canada?* I stood there with my eyes closed and stilled my mind, and to my relief, my hands started to move, the directions and energy coming from somewhere. Half an hour later, my hands stopped. The healing was finished. And wonder of wonders, Leanne said her back felt better; the pain was gone.

I was starting at the very basic level of discovery. What did I feel in my hands? Energy. What did I think was happening to the people I was healing? Their energy was changing. I did not need to know where the energy came from or how my hands knew where and how to move, but I did want to know what the energy did and how it worked. I knew that everything is made up of energy and that the molecular structure of our cells has an energy frequency. Therefore, I theorized, when we are unwell or injured, the frequency of the energy of the cells in that area slows down, no longer at an optimum level for health. And when I bring my hands to the unhealthy cells, they are infused with a high-frequency energy that brings them back up to an optimal energy level.

I wanted to know how the energy from my hands could heal people, but I also wanted to know how people could keep themselves in a higher frequency of energy so they could maintain their health. For days, months, and years I immersed my mind in the importance of energy. I started to look at the energy frequencies of our environment, our food, and our emotions, and how they can affect our health energy. Even though we can't see energy, we all know it's out there and that it can make physical matter change into radically different forms: ice to water to steam. This healing energy might be one we had little experience with, but it was still real. I sensed that if music, TV shows, art, and colour all have their own frequencies, then some will raise our energy and some will bring it down. The energy frequency of food depends on whether it is whole and organically grown, or heavily processed and grown with pesticides and herbicides. And our emotions and thoughts have their own frequencies, which greatly affect the frequency of energy in our bodies. Love and joy pull us up, fear and anger drag us down, and the ones in between affect us accordingly.

Within a few months of returning from England, I was working on quite a few people, mostly family. I was doing many small healings that got rid of the problem or pain in a single session. I was able to persevere despite my self-doubt only because of all the times people felt thoroughly healed after their session. I put very high demands on the healing, and expected an almost 100 percent success rate, preferably in one session. In my mind, if the healing I did wasn't going to be extraordinary, I wasn't interested in continuing, because I had never planned on being a healer anyway.

A healing I did on my dad is an example of a small healing that both of us found to be quite incredible. My dad was having a hard time walking because of extreme pain in his ankle. An X-ray had revealed that the cartilage in the joint was gone. The doctor advised him to come back in a week for a cortisone shot, as this was the only thing the doctor thought would be able to help. I went to my dad's house and the instant I touched his ankle, my hand started to move. I was far away in my thoughts as my hand moved around in different patterns on Dad's ankle. When the healing was over, Dad said it had been very intense and he had felt a lot of heat coming through my hands. Amazingly, this healing completely solved Dad's problem. The pain was gone, he didn't need the cortisone shot, and he never had trouble with the ankle again.

As time went on and I had the opportunity to undertake many different healings, my abilities expanded. Every now and then I would be shown an image or have a sense that a spirit was around. Images were especially useful because they helped me understand what was going on and I could describe the image to the person I was working with. I was shown images in a very simplistic form, such as a teacher might draw for a child. I was given all I needed to get the idea of what was happening.

Once, I was doing a healing on a man who was having trouble with his prostate and thought it might be enlarged. He had stayed overnight at our house, and when he woke up in the morning, he could not urinate at all. He was very anxious and wanted to go straight to the emergency department at the hospital. I suggested we do a healing first. With the man sitting facing me, I started to bring energy in through the top of his head and down through his body. As I got to his prostate, I had the image of an oblong balloon and I was told that the healing would be like taking some air out of the balloon so that urine could flow more easily through the urethra. This may seem overly simplified, but it was all the information I needed to know that the energy was working on the prostate. As soon as the healing was over, he went into the bathroom and he could pee just fine. He told me that as I had been helping to send energy to his prostate and visualizing the balloon deflating, he could feel his prostate shrinking. We had sat facing each other, eyes closed, not talking, but at the same time that I was seeing his prostate being healed, he was feeling it changing. It's amazing, but the proof is in the peeing.

I did healings whenever I had the chance, because I wanted to learn as much as I could about the potential of this newly discovered energy. So when Jeff skated off the ice in pain at a hockey tournament, I was ready to go to work. He had pulled a ligament in his groin. On the way home, he found it hard to get in and out of the car. He limped into the house and lay down, disappointed because he did not want to miss the game that afternoon. I saw in my mind's eye what looked like tape pulled up in the middle so it couldn't lay flat. As I worked on the area, the tape slowly began to flatten out. After about fifteen minutes, the tape was flat. My hand stopped moving and the images I was getting disappeared from my mind. Jeff was back in top form. He had some lunch and went off to his next game. We were both truly amazed.

I experienced a lot of inner conflict whenever I was trying to decide whether to open myself to doing a healing on someone other than the people closest to me. I felt vulnerable, but Spirit would often give me a sense that I should go ahead. I needed someone with me who could see and experience energy, who could witness the healings and verify what was going on. I had such an analytical mind that I wanted someone who could not only confirm my findings but also add greater insight. Working with Dana provided some of the validation I needed.

I wanted Dana to witness my healings and record everything she felt and saw. Dana's ability to see things such as auras was beneficial in increasing my understanding. She described the energy in different colours, sometimes as balls coming from my right hand. She also described energetic beings or spirits she saw in the room, either watching the healing or helping with it. She could feel my auric expansion, see the flow of energy from me into the person being healed, see the blocked energy, if there was any, and see it being removed.

One day she came to watch a healing I was doing on a young man who had problems with his hip. I sat down opposite him and we both closed our eyes. Dana later said that when I started the healing, she could see my aura expand and merge with this fellow's auric field. She also said that whenever I rocked forward or back or to the side, my patient did exactly the same thing. Even though we couldn't see each other, we moved in unison. Our energy linked us.

Dana and I worked together on healings with a number of people. She sensed the energy that I projected through my heart and head chakras. Chakras are energy vortices found at seven different locations running up the centre of the body and head. I see them as the conductors of energy, working on the physical, emotional, and spiritual levels. I had the sense that I could not only release energy through my hands but also stream it out of my chakras directly at the person being healed, without touching them. Dana and I tested this theory. I would send energy in streams to certain parts of her body, and Dana confirmed it. It was critical for me to have this proof that something real was taking place.

When Charlie returned from Russia, Dana could see his aura clearly. She said it was a dull grey, which indicated to Dana that his health was in serious trouble. He had endured some horrendous situations with bear poachers, and had given everything he had to complete the film with us and raise his bear cubs to independence. Now, more than anything else, I wanted to help Charlie get back on his feet. I started doing healings on him immediately. As I was doing the healing, I was amazed to see, coming through in spirit, two of the grizzly bears he had helped. They had come to help him in the healing, returning the love that he had so selflessly given them. They were kindred spirits and were there for each other on both sides of life. The healings gave Charlie the energy boost he needed so that his physical health improved, and Dana indicated his aura had regained a healthy colour.

About a year after I met Dana, she developed two herniated discs in her back. She was in intense pain. I did a few healings on her that relieved the pain for a while, but the discs remained herniated. Over the weeks, Dana's condition declined rapidly. She took to walking with a cane, began losing consciousness and falling, and her left leg was going numb. She went in for a scan and the medical team said they had to take immediate action. They scheduled an MRI for a week later, after which the surgeon would operate. They said she could not wait or she might not walk again. Dana called me to say she was definitely going ahead with the operation— she was scared and couldn't risk not having it.

That week, I drove the two hours to Dana's house to do healings on her. I streamed energy down through the top of her head and into her body. Every time I brought the energy down, it seemed to stop at her heart chakra, the vortex of energy movement around the heart and chest. This was the first time I could sense a chakra and feel the blockage that was created because it was not open. Dana could feel the energy stop there as well, which was welcome confirmation that I was sensing the energy correctly. I kept bringing the energy down until I finally felt it move through and her heart chakra began to flow with energy again. I felt that this movement was critical in order to get the energy to her herniated discs, which were in her lower lumbar region.

At this time, I saw the need to get the energy moving only as a physical issue. I didn't comprehend the deep connection between Dana's blocked chakra and the emotional pain from her past that needed to be energetically released in order to allow a healthy energy frequency throughout her body, especially up and down her spine. We needed to clear the energy in order for the physical healing to occur. But if I had only worked directly on the disc area, without bringing the energy down through her head, I would have missed healing the heart chakra. Then the healing to her discs might not have worked, and it certainly would not have lasted, because high-frequency energy would still not have been able to flow through her. Her energy would have steadily declined again, creating more problems in her spine or other areas.

I did not realize at the time how important the healing of her heart chakra was to the success of her overall healing. I was being shown something very significant about the heart chakra, but I did not yet recognize it.

I did four daily healings on her that week, but I had no sense whether they were helping. On the fifth day, I called Dana to say I was coming over, but she told me not to. She said the healing was finished, that my job was done. She described a dream she had had the night before in which she was lying on a white marble table and I was standing in the background in a long robe. Her guides and some spirit beings were around her. They told her, "Sue has finished the healing. Now you just have to accept it into your body."

Dana meditated that day to accept the healing. I wasn't sure what that meant, but it seemed very important.

The next day, she went for her MRI and met with the surgeon. After the appointment, she called me, ecstatic beyond belief. The surgery had been cancelled. The MRI showed that the discs were no longer herniated and her back was entirely healthy. The doctor could not explain what had occurred. Dana hadn't mentioned anything to the doctor about the energy work we had done together. Shocked and excited, we knew that this had huge implications for the healing work I was doing. It was indisputable that energy could change a physical condition and that higher frequencies of energy, when allowed to flow freely, could heal. And it was clear that I could conduct that energy; the difference between the scan and the MRI was proof.

Jeff and I phoned Charlie with the news about Dana, and he was equally thrilled. Charlie was very interested in the healings and liked to think outside the box. Everything he had learned about bears was due to his ability to entertain notions that went beyond conventional wisdom. He didn't see this healing as "foo-foo"; this was energy creating change.

This experience with Dana gave us lots to think about and raised many questions. How did the healing take place? How was it possible to heal two herniated discs? And most importantly, what did Dana do to accept the healing or the energy into her body? How did she allow the healing to take place? We were grateful to experience what we thought of as a miracle, but really, it was just something beyond our limited perspective. Catching a glimpse of what is possible motivated me to keep trying and experimenting with more healing.

I feel that I'm being shown something; I'm being guided to an understanding. The energy is much bigger than the healings. The healings are profound, but they're showing us glimpses of the possibilities for something much bigger, something I believe is obtainable by us all. The hardest thing for me on this journey is to trust and have faith. Not faith in the energy—I believe its abundance and power are limitless—but faith in myself, that I can muster the courage for this journey and that I can, in some way, reflect this energy so others can experience it and see the possibilities.

Energy lets us witness physical change, because as human beings in a physical world, this is what we can most relate to. But the role of this energy is to take us to the emotional level. Energy enables us to connect to the vibrational rate of our emotions, their physical implications, and the profound effect they have on other people, animals, and the Earth.

This healing brought Dana and me even closer together. She could truly appreciate what was happening and had a great deal of respect for it. I needed people around me who wanted to share in this larger-than-life experience, and I felt that they were few. I didn't want family and friends to feel awkward around me. Some people fairly close to me were so uncomfortable with what Dana did as a medium—communicating with Spirit, which could be as simple as having a chat with their deceased grandma—that they never wanted to meet her, talk about what she did, or acknowledge my friendship with her. And what I was doing was much more unusual than talking to our departed loved ones.

As a medium, Dana was a bridge between the physical world and the spiritual world, which we can't readily perceive. She also helped me deal with the pain of losing loved ones. When Hazel passed away, I was devastated. Chelsea also felt the loss deeply. Dana came to visit a couple of days after we had received the news. She hadn't known Hazel or heard much about her, but while we were sitting in the living room, Dana said she saw Hazel dancing for us. Dana did not know that Hazel had been a dancer when she was young in India, and had performed with other dancers in concerts to raise money to help injured soldiers during the war. Hazel had shown Chelsea and me pictures of herself onstage. It made us so happy that she was with us and dancing again.

Hazel stayed and talked, through Dana, for quite a while. She said her life review had gone well. A life review is an assessment of the life you have just lived, looking at the choices you made and how you affected everyone you interacted with. She wanted to reassure Chelsea and me that she would continue to be with us and help us in our lives as much as she could.

Dana made the spirit world seem a part of who we are, instead of something oddly separate.

CLARA AND JOE'S LASTING LOVE

ALTHOUGH I HAD no doubt that a gifted medium like Dana received very accurate information from people who had left the physical, I was somewhere between believing and disbelieving that it was possible for me to connect with Spirit and get messages. I was always testing myself, because I wanted to err on the side of caution. This was my state of mind as I sat among the heather on an alpine mountaintop high above Whistler, British Columbia.

While Jeff was filming scenic shots and looking for black bears, I decided to enjoy the peaceful beauty and solitude of the high country. But as I relaxed and let my mind go, into my awareness came Jeff's aunt Clara. She seemed to want to give me a message. She had passed away a few years earlier, of a melanoma by her right eye. Now she was giving me the feeling that she wanted me to offer healing to her husband, Joe.

Joe, now eighty-five years old, was a lively Italian man with a big smile. He and Clara had been married for fifty-four years. Joe had once told me that the first time he saw Clara, with her beautiful blond hair and blue eyes, he wanted to marry her. Joe loved bonsai trees and had about twenty growing in little pots in his back garden. He used to grow peppers and tomatoes using hydroponics in a greenhouse. After Clara's passing, Joe lived alone. For all the years since her death, he had kept her ashes in an urn on his fireplace mantel with a candle burning beside them.

Joe had called me months before, when Jeff was filming in Russia, to ask how Jeff was doing and if he was finding any bears. Clara had cared deeply for animals and had donated money to conservation groups, and she and Joe had always been very keen on our wildlife films. Every time we flew out from Vancouver to a film location, Uncle Joe would drive us to the airport so we could park our truck at their house while we were gone. On our return, Clara and Joe always welcomed us at the arrival gate. Jeff had lived with them when he was going to university, so they shared a special connection.

Joe wanted to know how Jeff was coping with the challenges of filming in such a remote location. After we had talked about Jeff, Joe started to tell me about his health problems. He had a bad hip, his spine hurt, he was having trouble with his kidneys and gallbladder, and the circulation in his legs was so bad that they were discoloured from the knees down. I hadn't talked to Joe in years and was surprised he would phone me and speak so openly about his ailments.

As usual, I kept my cards about healing close to my chest. Our extended family would, I felt, have the hardest time thinking of me in these terms, because this was so far from the person any of them thought I was.

But now Clara was with me on the mountaintop, bringing up Joe and his health. She was concerned about him and seemed to be asking if I could help him with healing. I thought this would be a big leap of faith for Joe, who seemed such a traditional guy. So I wanted to be sure of the message I felt I was getting from Clara before I talked to Joe.

The only way I could think to do this was to ask Clara to give Dana a message. If Dana received a visit from Clara, not knowing anything about it from me, it would confirm that I really had talked to Clara, and I would have the courage to call Joe and offer healing. I realize this sounds like a convoluted way of going about things, but I always needed more proof.

I decided to wait a couple of days before calling Dana, to give Clara the time she needed to get her message across. Dana could not contact me because we had cellphone reception only when we went into town.

A couple of days later, when we were on our way to Vancouver, I had the strongest urge to call Dana right away. I asked if she had any unexpected spirits around her that she couldn't explain. She did have a spirit with her, she said. She didn't know who it was, but it was female. Dana said that this woman had died from a disease. She then asked if this person had something wrong with her right eye, because Dana had taken on the symptoms of the woman and her eye had got red and sore. And then, getting a little exasperated, she said that she also felt nauseated, as if she were on chemotherapy. She could tell that the spirit with her was a woman who had died from cancer that had affected her right eye.

I had the evidence I needed. Clara had been able to contact me as I sat on a coastal mountain, ask for my help for Joe, and then, at my request, go to Dana in the interior of British Columbia and give her enough information to easily identify her. And then she had waited for me to connect with Dana. It was a wonderful circle.

As soon as I had spoken to Dana, Clara left her alone. Dana's eye cleared immediately and her nausea disappeared. Dana had experienced these symptoms for a couple of days, and I think I tested her patience a little by waiting to call. I didn't know Clara would be such a fast traveller. But what was I thinking? It's not as though she had to take the bus.

I phoned Joe and asked if we could stop by for a visit. When we got to his home, I sat with him at his kitchen table. I told my story of healing and asked if he would like to give it a try—maybe I could alleviate some of his discomfort. He was eager to give it a go and in no way seemed surprised. Perhaps Clara had given him a heads-up.

We sat across from each other while I sent energy to him through my chakras without touching him. Joe said it felt as though he had electricity running down his legs, and his left leg actually jumped off the floor twice, lifting his foot by about three inches. He was impressed and so was I. The energy worked down through his body and down his legs. After that healing, I worked on his spine, lower back, and left hip and leg with my hands-on healing. I got no movement in my hand on his right leg. I guess that was not where the work was needed.

Afterwards, Joe and I went for a walk and he said that he was finding it much easier to climb stairs. I asked him if he would like another healing in a few days or a week. He said it felt so good, he would like one every day! I came back one more time, but to really help him I thought we would need a series of sessions, every day for at least a couple of weeks. I couldn't be in Vancouver that long and Joe didn't want to leave home and travel to Whistler.

Joe called me a few weeks later to say he had been able to go out with a friend into the coastal forest and look for new bonsai trees. He had walked with ease and enjoyed the outing so much. He hadn't thought he would ever be able to indulge that love of his again. I was pleased to have been able to help him with that small blessing.

I thank Clara for having patience with me and believing in me enough to make this time with Joe possible. Although physically Joe didn't make a big recovery, on a spiritual level it meant a great deal to him to know that Clara was still around, that her love was very much with him, and that his feelings about her still being there were correct. This gave him more strength than a good pair of legs.

Joe has now left the physical world and is with Clara, enjoying the biggest bonsai garden he could ever have imagined.

CONSCIOUS EVOLUTION

THROUGH ALL THE healings, I had the sense that I was being taught about the many levels of energy—physical, emotional, and spiritual—and that this understanding was leading me towards a greater and richer understanding of life. But I was not always sure of the steps to take to further my development, so I tried to be open to any opportunity that came my way. I never knew when something would show up or how it would come to me. I was becoming much more sensitive to Spirit, and that was really helpful. But sometimes messages would catch me by surprise.

On a beautiful sunny day, I was having lunch with Jeff at the Vancouver Art Gallery. We were sitting outside at the little café, having a lovely time. Then, unexpectedly, I saw the cover of a book in my mind's eye. It was titled *Conscious Evolution*. I instantly knew this was a message from Spirit suggesting that I write a book, a thought that had never before crossed my mind.

I realized that *Conscious Evolution* didn't need to be the actual title of the book I would write, but thinking about those two words gave me insights into understanding energy in a new way. When I saw the title, there was an understanding that this was about consciously evolving on an emotional level. It had nothing to do with the physical development that we normally think of when we hear the word "evolution."

When we are conscious of only the physical world around us, we tend to view ourselves as singular. This sense of being separate from each other brings with it feelings of competition, greed, jealousy, judgment, anger, and so on—all emotions resulting from fear. As a species, we continue to segregate ourselves by countries, religions, races, genders, and any other label we can find. The fear-based emotions that stem from a life lived mainly in the energies of the physical, seeing ourselves as strictly physical beings, lead us to make choices that create the very circumstances that threaten to destroy our planet and ourselves.

But if we start to see ourselves not only as physical beings but as emotional and spiritual energies, then we can change the way we think about our future. I believe we all possess three energy layers. First, we have our physical body and the energy at which it vibrates. Then, just beyond that, we have our emotional body, which vibrates at different energy frequencies depending on what we are feeling. Finally, surrounding that, we have our spiritual body, which resonates with energies that are connected to our higher self and the spiritual or soul connection we have to the universe.

By thinking of ourselves as having different energy bodies, we can choose to consciously evolve. Our emotional body experiences a wide range of sensations, from fear to love. If we think of ourselves as having this emotional energy around us, we can work at trying to move away from emotions such as anger, shame, jealousy, resentment, and blame towards emotions of understanding, joy, gratitude, and love.

I believe we are meant to use our emotions as a guidance system in making choices. The language of our spiritual being is how we feel. Our soul's path communicates with us by how we feel about the choices we are making. We can't always intellectualize why we are drawn to certain choices, but if they are made because of joy, excitement, and love, then we are most likely on the right track.

Our spiritual bodies mostly resonate with the energy of love and compassion. We can consciously choose to live spiritually in a state of love and compassion in every decision we make—the food we eat, the products we use, our interactions with others, and so on. You can be loving and compassionate while experiencing different emotions. I have felt great love and compassion at times when I was suffering from depression. Being a loving and compassionate person doesn't translate to always feeling joyful, peppy, and positive. But I think that making a decision to be in a spiritual energetic state of love and compassion will directly affect the state of our health and the Earth. Because our emotions are energy waves that go out from us and interact with the world, it's not hard to appreciate that we are connected. Since all matter is really just a form of energy, the way we interact with the energy of our environment and the people in our circle has a huge impact on our own well-being and that of everything around us. When we understand that we are not separate from each other, from the animals, or from the Earth, and that our energy is very much interconnected, then we will also understand that what is good for us is good for the whole, and vice versa. I think we are entering a time in the evolution of our planet where if we learn to listen to how we feel about the choices we make, we can begin to live with the emotional and spiritual energies we desire. I had what I consider an idyllic young life. My family—my mom, my dad, three older sisters, and many pets—and I lived in the Canadian wilderness, in a small log home at the end of a meadow surrounded by a beautiful forest. For a child, it was the perfect setting.

Our little house was very basic. We did not have electricity, running water, or indoor plumbing. This meant that as a family we sat around a single kerosene lamp on winter nights, reading, writing, or talking. It meant collecting water from the little creek that ran past our back door and having baths in a small tin tub in front of the wood stove in the kitchen. It also meant walking about a hundred metres into the trees to the outhouse, with the chance of visiting a bear along the way. It made for a life rich in experience and adventure.

Our land was situated in a narrow river valley with forested mountains on either side. We had no neighbours within a radius of a few kilometers. There was a small village downriver from us with about a hundred people, one little store, and a post office that was in an elderly lady's home. My grandparents and uncle lived in this little town, and we were very close. We were the third generation in this area, which made us one of the older families. Those years fill me with happy memories.

On our small farm we had a horse named Flicka, a cow named Blondie, pigs, chickens, rabbits, and a fantastic collie dog named Tag. There were also many wild animals around, including deer, coyotes, cougars, and black bears. The bears would come all around our house; I can even remember them on our porch. We were never taught to be afraid of them. My mom especially loved animals, and she taught us to have a great deal of respect for all creatures. She encouraged us to think of animals, birds, and insects from their point of view, to try to imagine what they thought and felt. We often raised orphaned birds and animals that we found or that other people brought to us. One robin that we raised came back to us every spring for many years and had her own family in a nest above our living room window. My dad once brought home a nest of flying squirrel babies that he had found in a fallen tree. Both my parents made nature our home, and for that I am most grateful.

We kept our daily expenses low, living mainly off our large vegetable garden and meat from farm animals or wild animals. Every fall my dad would head into the mountains on horseback to hunt in hopes of getting a deer. When he came back, I would run to meet him to see if he had been successful. We also hunted grouse. I have a strong memory of helping to pluck grouse feathers behind our house and playing with the gizzards, the tiny sacks of pebbles in their necks that help them break down their food. They were like Hacky Sacks.

I don't remember the deaths of these animals, nor do I recall the deaths of any farm animals; my parents must have shielded me from those traumatic situations. This was how we lived, and as a child I never knew there was any other way.

By the time I was in high school, my life had changed a great deal. My sisters had gone to colleges far away and my parents had separated. By my early teens, I was becoming very independent and a free thinker. I never resented my parents for their decision to live apart. I understood that times and people change.

Today that sentiment is more and more meaningful. I hope that most people are able to change with the easily accessible new knowledge and a quickly changing planet. I have found that one of the biggest obstacles for people trying to change is their ties to their culture and to their family's accepted ways of doing things. They can let this get in the way of their own healing process. A lot of what we do as a society is based on the way we have always done it, and this is detrimental to our health and to the well-being of other animals and the planet. Our population is growing so quickly that the cumulative impact is staggering.

It's interesting to me that even though our grandmothers didn't have cellphones or the Internet, we happily embrace these rapid technological changes. Most people love change and learning new things, especially when it makes their lives easier—as cellphones do. But other types of change, such as altering our diet, seem to deter a lot of people, as they require a perceived sacrifice. I say "perceived," because a lot of times I find that when you make the change, it's not as much of a sacrifice as it appeared.

Many years ago, when we were in England, Jeff and I went with some friends to a pub to have a few drinks and something to eat. I ordered cod and chips because that's what I always had at pubs in the UK and I loved it. The man we were with asked me if I realized that Atlantic cod were endangered. I knew then that I had made a poor choice, and that was the last time I had fish and chips. Traditions are fun and comforting because they allow us to know what to expect in our lives, but there are some that no longer serve us well. To evolve on an emotional level and make choices from a place of love and compassion requires us to think about which traditions to hold on to and which to abandon.

My family, like most, came from generations of people who had certain ways of living and never thought about change. They did not have access to the resources most of us have today or to information that would have let them understand the world differently. But I know that my grandparents' lifestyle didn't entirely work for them, because three of them died from cancer. We are members of another generation, with many new choices. Let's keep the old patterns that are harmless and let the others go the way of Morse code. A cellphone is so much easier.

I loved my childhood, but when we brought up Chelsea and Logan, Jeff and I decided to do some things differently than our parents had. And our children themselves brought their own ideas for change into our lives. It was Chelsea who decided, at the age of ten, after studying a book she discovered in a bookstore in England, that we should be vegetarians. Her reasons made sense, the information she found transformed our thinking, and as a family we changed our diet, first to vegetarian and then to vegan. We have over the years established new traditions that blend with some of the old ways of doing things. I am so happy that both of my kids are capable of thinking for themselves and that they realize they are creating the world in which they live.

STARTING FROM BASE CAMP

Pat

CHARLIE CALLED TO ask if I would be interested in doing a healing for his friend Pat. Before he could finish his sentence, every fibre of my being was saying, "Yes, yes, yes." It's astounding how some things feel so right and you don't know why—intuition, rather than a conscious decision. My spirit guides must have been mighty pleased about our connection, because I had no doubt about Pat coming for healing.

I didn't know Pat, and would learn later that he had lived an incredible life. He was the first person to climb to the highest summit on every continent, an accomplishment for which he was appointed to the Order of Canada. He has also written many books and is a very successful photographer and filmmaker. He lived for a long time in the Himalayas, climbing, hiking, filming, and experiencing the spirituality of the culture.

Although Pat had been an extreme athlete, Charlie said he was now doing very poorly. A year or so earlier, he had collapsed while on a routine hike in the Rockies. He thought he had suffered a heart attack, but a prolonged series of tests confirmed it had been an esophageal spasm, which produces symptoms nearly identical to those of a heart attack. He couldn't shake the belief that his collapse had something to do with his cardiac system, on which he had depended so heavily for his many high-mountain adventures. It was hard for him to sit up for long, walk very far, or even read a book. He had been to doctors and tried many alternative treatments, but nothing helped.

I talked to Pat on the phone. He was soft-spoken and seemed peaceful. He said he would come to my home and treat the experience as a healing retreat. He would devote the whole of himself to the healing and would bring no other work or have any other agenda. Pat was the first person to come to me who wasn't friend or family, and at the time I had no idea how blessed I was to work with him. He was gentle, kind, unassuming, humble, and utterly devoted to the healing, and he showed me complete respect. I was in a vulnerable position, opening myself up to a stranger. But with the healing, there is no room for self-consciousness—I have to completely let myself go and fully trust the process, and it is critical that the person I'm doing the healing with can let go and trust as well. Pat trusted.

Pat and Baiba, his partner and wife, were soon on their way, driving about ten hours to our house. In the early morning I dreamed that they were coming down the highway in a Subaru. I had never known anyone with a Subaru, so it seemed like an interesting detail. That evening they arrived in a Subaru.

Pat, Baiba, and my family sat together in our living room to get acquainted. Pat looked drained; his colouring and energy were diminished. Baiba did the talking, as Pat was tired. Although Pat was a stranger when he arrived, I felt so much joy and energy at the thought of helping him with healing. When you are connected with your soul's journey, I think, you cannot help but feel joyful.

The next day, Baiba left and Pat and I began our journey. Jeff had set up a healing area in our basement. It was quite nice, but it was underground, in the back corner of a room with cement walls, beside the furnace and the hot water heater. My healing table (like a massage table) was there and we had decorated the space to look somewhat special.

The first morning, my hands moved readily. Something was happening, but I had no visions or messages and no sense of what might be wrong with Pat's health. I did a type of healing in which I sit in front of the person and send energy to them through my heart chakra, first opening their root chakra and working up to their crown chakra. I then bring energy down through the person to the areas that need healing. On this first day, I received no clues from the spirit world or my guides about what was wrong with Pat.

That night I lay awake for hours, feeling alone and scared. I was out of my element. Maybe I had taken on too much. Pat was obviously very sick, and I did not feel equipped to handle something this serious. After all, if I were an authentic healer, wouldn't I be able to look into his body, see exactly what was wrong, and then give him a report of my findings? I was sure a real healer could pinpoint the problem in this way.

The next morning, I decided to get the healing table out of the basement. It felt so closed in down there. I needed to feel lighter, with the brightness of the outside world. Jeff and

I moved the table into our large upstairs bathroom, which had a six-foot-wide bay window and French doors. Although it wasn't perfect, it was above ground.

The healing that morning seemed very busy, with lots of energy movement, but I still was given no information. I had to have faith in an energy source I didn't understand and couldn't explain. Energy was coming through me. My hands moved in patterns and tapped in rhythms. Why they went where they did, with the movements they did, I mostly didn't understand. I had to think about something else during the treatments. I was scared that if I thought about what I was doing, I would screw it up; my mind would judge my actions and that might get in the way of the healing.

The healings lasted from twenty to forty minutes, and then they would stop. I would scan Pat's body with my hand open, palm down, to see if the movement would start again. When the healing was over, I would feel absolutely no more movement. The movement all comes through my right hand. My left hand takes certain still positions on the body and seems to have a more direct connection to the person.

I decided to do two healings a day on Pat for about ten days. It was an intuitive decision.

In the early afternoon, I felt as though I needed a sauna and some meditation. I was feeling intimidated and insecure. Pat was very unwell and I wanted some assurance I wasn't wasting his time, a sign or some sort of message from the spirit world to give me courage to go on.

I changed into my bathing suit and was just settling into the sauna when Logan arrived and asked if he could join me. I was pleased to have his company but said I was doing a meditation so we wouldn't be talking.

I went into a deep meditation fairly easily. I asked anyone in the spirit world that came in love to please come forth and help me. *I am desperate and I need assistance. Please. I am trusting and have faith, but I need something.* I didn't have an expectation of what message I might get, but I was open.

I then saw the most beautiful image of Jesus. He stood before me with his hands open, extended one hand, and pulled me to my feet towards him. I had a strong sensation that he was there to help. He looked into my eyes for a few minutes and then was gone. I don't know how long I meditated, but when I opened my eyes, Logan was watching me intently. He said I had gone completely limp and my head had fallen over. It had looked as if I had stopped breathing and he had watched me carefully to see if I moved at all. Detecting the smallest breath, he had decided he shouldn't disturb me. But he was relieved to see me back with him in consciousness.

I didn't know what had happened. My hope when I had asked for help was that I would meet one of my spirit guides, or maybe my grandmother would come through to tell me everything was okay. The last thing in the world I expected or would even have contemplated was seeing an image of Jesus. But whatever happened, seeing him filled me with an abundance of energy and renewed courage to carry on with the healing.

I have never been religious. Praying to God or Jesus was not part of my practice. Although I would say that I believe Jesus lived and was an incredible person, I was not raised in a traditional faith and my experience with religion has not been encouraging. It seems much too segregating, instead of bringing humanity together as one. And some religions seem to be based much more on fear than on love. God, to me, is unconditional love for everyone. And therefore Jesus would personify this love, which doesn't judge and decide whom to shine on.

A surprising situation I experienced as a child got me thinking about religion at quite an early age. When I was about seven years old, a girl came up to me after school and told me I should pack my things that night and run away from home, come to her house. She said that everyone on Earth was going to die except for the people in her church. I lived about ten kilometres away from her house, so the thought of that walk in the dark didn't appeal to me. But more importantly, from my point of view, my family was truly wonderful. My mom, the local schoolteacher, was always helping others. It didn't make sense to me that this girl's family was worth saving and mine wasn't. I didn't believe it could be true. So I decided to stay with my family.

When I was about twenty, a friend came to me for help late one night. A friend of hers, who had tried to take her life, was in the hospital. My friend wanted me to come and speak to her. I spent a few hours talking with the young woman. I felt very comfortable helping her, and giving her love and support came naturally to me. When we left, my girlfriend anxiously tried to convince me to join her church. She said I was one of the most loving and caring people she had ever known, but unless I joined her church and accepted Jesus into my life, I would not be saved.

Both of these friends who tried to save me acted from a good place, what they believed to be true. But I think the messages that have been passed down have been so misunderstood and our interpretations so misguided that they can ruin the words and actions of a profound man. I believe that Jesus's love is for all, and religion does not come into it. I think that when people say we will be saved if we accept Jesus into our lives, what is really meant is that if we strive to live more in his form of love and compassion, we will lift ourselves up to a place where suffering does not exist. I would say that the word "accept" could be replaced by "become more like," and "to be saved" could be "to transcend our suffering to attain a state of well-being."

Pat and I had daily sessions of healing, and I could now see images of energy movement inside his body. I was able to let go of the need to know exactly what was wrong in any one spot; in its place was the sense of healing the whole. I could clearly see I needed to raise the vibrational frequency of *all* the cells, as they, like everything else, are interconnected.

When I was working on an area of the body that had residual emotional energy, I would often experience strong emotions myself. I believe that as I healed Pat, I released the emotion that was causing the vibrational decline and creating the illness. The sensations would stream through me, causing me to feel very emotional. Some would say I should have blocked myself from these energies so that they wouldn't affect me, but at this point in my experience I felt a need to open myself to the emotions I was uncovering in order to fully understand the process of the healing.

The person I am working with often does not experience the magnitude of emotion or detail of feeling that I do. They are usually in a deeply relaxed state or sleeping. There is a direct correlation between the seriousness of the disease and how much emotion and excess energy I experience.

The lower the rate of the energy in the cells, the greater the release or effect on me as the vibrational rate of the cells increases and comes back to a state of wellness. But this happens only at certain stages in the healing.

During one healing, Pat was sitting in a chair when I saw Jesus standing behind him. He had his hands on Pat's shoulders. I pulled streams of energy out of Jesus's fingers in a diagonal pattern across Pat's chest. I didn't need to talk to Jesus in sentences; I had just the glimpse of a thought and I immediately had the answer from him.

Because we see the image in our mind's eye—this is how many mediums work—for those of us who are only used to the physical world it takes some sensitivity to be open and go with it. I decided to take Pat to see Dana so that she could observe a healing. I wanted to see if she had a sense of how the healings were going and if she could offer any insights. Also, I asked the spirit world, if the images I had of Jesus were real, could he please show himself to Dana?

As I was doing the healing with Dana present, Jesus once again appeared to me. I was very excited and grateful, but I did not react in any way—I wanted confirmation from Dana. When the healing was complete, I looked over at her. She was wide-eyed and said, "You're never going to believe this, but, but— Maybe I shouldn't mention it ... I know it sounds crazy, but I saw Jesus."

It was such an affirmation for me to have Dana, whom I deeply respected as a medium, witness the same image. She said, "He looked at me and smiled."

We shared this experience with Pat. I think it was a bit of a stretch for him, as it would be for many people. It sure would be for me if I hadn't seen it myself. Pat was gracious and did not seem to judge us.

Now, long after my experience with Pat, I don't tell most people I work with if I have a vision of Jesus during their healing. Energy healing is a lot for most people to get their head around. If I add that their deceased mother is in the room talking to me, it is quite a bit more for them to conceive of; so telling them that Jesus is there feels way over the top. I have, for the most part, kept these visions a secret, and I even feel uncomfortable writing about them in this book—it is so unlike anything I would have imagined happening to me on this path. If I were writing a movie script, I would never add this in, because, as they say, it would be too on the nose.

Years after my first visualization of Jesus, a renowned teacher and psychic medium from Scotland told me I was seeing Christ energy in a form I could recognize. Christ energy is one of the highest frequencies of energy and one of the highest forms of love, and, therefore, is intensely healing. The spirit realm shows me an image of Jesus so I can understand, in my limited capacity, the magnitude of the healing energy that is possible. As with many of the experiences I've had on my spiritual journey, the message comes in the feeling and emotion I experience with the image. I have decided in recent years not to over-analyze the images I've had of Jesus. They are inspirational images that fill me with a great sense of love. I accept them as that.

On the last day of healing, Pat was back to a state of well-being. It had been a gradual process, with Pat improving incrementally each day. All the tightness in his chest was gone, his colour looked good, and his energy was back.

For me, this was a model healing. All the truths I had been compiling seemed to unfold and come together to complete the healing. Pat's open and non-judgmental way of being, and his gratitude for this amazing energy of light and love, allowed the healing to be so successful.

On the morning Pat was leaving, he, Jeff, Chelsea, Logan, Charlie, and I stood together in the kitchen. I hugged Charlie and thanked him for bringing Pat into my life. Then Pat, looking bright and energized, a completely different person from the one who had arrived nine days earlier, hugged me and said, "Thank you for giving me back my life."

Being part of such a profound experience with Pat was a blessing and a gift, one of the highlights of my life. I thank the universe for bringing him into my life, and I thank him for allowing himself to come and for embracing the healing with heart and soul. I felt that if I never had a chance to heal again, what I had experienced would be enough. It felt truly me, my truth.

THE COLLEGE FOR MEDIUMS

NOT LONG AFTER I met her, Dana travelled to England to attend the Arthur Findlay College for mediumship and returned with countless stories. It made total sense that Dana would go to this prestigious college; she was a very accomplished medium. But when she asked if I would go with her when she went back, I thought she was completely daft. I was not a medium. I sensed spirits sometimes and felt I got some messages, but I didn't think I was student material for Arthur Findlay College. But somehow Dana convinced me to go for a week.

We slept in the dorms, ate in the dining hall, were assigned to tutors, and went to our classes. I'm too much of a free spirit to enjoy much structure and being told what to do, but I decided to give it my best. We did a lot of psychic exercises, most of which I was not very good at. To do well psychically, I have to be as close to my true self as possible, and sitting in a classroom does not take me there. But what an amazing place it was, and what extraordinary mediums taught there. Seldom had I witnessed such clear and beautiful energy links with the spirit world.

What I experienced at the college was unforgettable. I watched mediums work in front of audiences, connecting to friends and family who had passed and speaking on their behalf for ten to fifteen minutes without stopping. Can you imagine that much information being delivered through a medium from an energy form no longer in the physical—and it's all accurate and makes sense? I could have attended those sessions for hours. I also saw mediums go into deep trances and allow a spiritual energy to enter their energy field and speak through them directly. For an hour, another energy being would talk to us about matters of importance to humankind from the perspective of another energy dimension. It was real, it was mind-bending, and it offered unimaginable insights into the universe.

We also watched Brazilian trance medium painter José Medrado channel artists such as Monet, Van Gogh, and Renoir and paint images of their art, within minutes. It was such a gift to be in the company of people so accomplished in connecting with energy in spirit form. When you see it in person, it changes you forever; you can never experience your own physical life in the same way again.

On a personal level, I had readings and discussions with mediums at the college who helped me a great deal in appreciating my own energy and in seeing possible paths in my journey. It gave me a boost of confidence that all I was sensing and believing did have meaning.

On our last day at the college, we each were to get up in front of the class and give a medium reading for one of the other students. I had absolutely no idea if I could connect and give a message. When it was my turn, all I could hear in my head was to do my best and not worry. As I stood in front of the other students and two instructional mediums, I saw, in my mind's eye, an older woman standing before me. She was wearing a flowered cotton dress, her hand was resting on a counter, and she had some rings on one finger. The skin around the rings had puffed up and it looked as if she couldn't take them off. The details of the image amazed me. Then I saw the word "cancer" and I knew she had died of cancer. Next I saw the word "pancreas."

When I described the woman and the cancer, Dana raised her hand. She said she believed it was her grandmother. The woman was giving me the feeling she was bringing a lot of love, but strangely, it felt that she was giving the love to me, not to Dana. Dana said her grandmother had always given the other children in the family more attention than she gave her. I saw daffodils and other images that made sense to Dana. Then I saw a map of Europe and, next, Dana packing up her belongings in Canada and putting them in the trunk of her car. I said it looked as though Dana would be travelling to Europe. Maybe she was going on a tour to demonstrate her work as a medium. Dana's grandmother faded away, and that seemed to be the end of my demonstration. The energy from connecting to this lady pumped me up and I was excited beyond measure at this success.

Looking back, I think Dana's grandmother was sending me love because she knew I would need it. What she knew, but I didn't, was that Dana had decided to cut all ties to Canada and move to England. Dana had connected to England in a deep way and wanted to start fresh in life. She moved suddenly, leaving her husband and her friends and changing her name.

We have spoken on the phone a couple of times and she has given me phone readings about people I am healing.

She seems very happy and I hope her journey is on track for what she needs to accomplish. We are good friends and she helped me a great deal with my own development.

Dana's leaving was a huge loss for me. I missed her greatly as a friend, confidante, and teacher. She was a kindred spirit on my path and one of the few people with whom I could truly be myself. I never felt judgment from her, only someone cheering me on. And that is a wonderful kind of person to have in your life.

As I write this, I'm smiling. I think it was rather fitting that the spirit world connected Dana and me at the beginning of our friendship and then brought through the message of her departure.

MY OWN PATH

THIS JOURNEY HAS often felt lonely, but I realize this has been partly my own doing. I was trying to keep my healing ability hidden from most people because I continued to fear judgment. I felt I was walking a thin and shaky line. I had many insecurities and weaknesses, so my deepest thoughts and inspirations remained my biggest secret. I feared that maybe I was wrong about my own abilities. Doing healings and studying energy seemed to be such an incredible long shot; it was not something I had even remotely imagined in my life.

Of course, Jeff, Chelsea, and Logan were right there with me, always supportive of the healings and my discoveries. But I wanted some authoritative figure to tell me beyond any doubt that I was on the right track. My ego self (my sense of myself in my mind) wanted me to give it up, to take the easy road and keep my blinders on. But my inner self (the sense of myself through my soul) kept pushing me on, not wanting me to stop and making me feel despair at the thought of quitting. I would become physically ill and depressed at even the idea of giving up. The drive was relentless.

On a soul level, this was everything I lived for. But on a day-to-day level, it just seemed to complicate my life. The healings were, at times, very demanding, taking everything I had to give. They were fulfilling, but also required a great effort on my part. Still, I always had a sense that I would completely miss the point of this lifetime if I didn't keep putting one foot in front of the other, going in the direction of understanding what these higher energies mean to us as humans.

Through these early years, I searched for someone who could give me the answers I needed for my journey. I had many readings from psychic mediums. One told me that my spirit guides couldn't tell me what was in my future because it would be too frightening. Another said there were no books I could study or courses I could take because where I was going was uncharted territory. Another medium told me that my grandparents were there, telling her that, just as they had been pioneers who blazed a trail across new land in the physical world, I would blaze a trail in the spiritual world.

I think early on I desperately wanted someone to describe the journey so I could decide if making the trip would be worthwhile. I still struggle with what it takes to walk this path, but I've learned over the years that I need to be still and listen carefully to what my soul is telling me. It has the answers I need and will guide me where I need to go. The hardest thing is trusting in myself and not letting fear get in the way. If I live in the moment, focusing on what I need to do next, the moment is not fearful, but if I get ahead of myself, I can find the fear. Our soul guides us in the present moment, and that's all we really need to know.

Although I have read some incredible books and learned from some wonderful teachers, I felt that too much information might limit my growth somehow. I needed to feel my way and discover my own understanding of these experiences, not live on the periphery of other people's information or be influenced by their opinions. So it has been a huge privilege to find my own path and, in doing so, bring my own perspective to everything I have learned.

I am a practical and straightforward person. In taking a world that seems untouchable and mystical and making it graspable, I have created a place where I can rediscover my connection to my true self.

TAKING TIME TO HEAL

Ellen

LLEN CAME TO me because she had a cancerous tumour growing by her liver. Doctors couldn't operate because of the way it was attached, and they'd told her she had a year to live.

I never spend much time listening to details of my patients' diseases. I do not want to hold the energy of my thoughts there, because I want to move on to the vibration of health. I also find that people are quick to take on the disease as part of their identity, and this thought process is dangerous and self-fulfilling.

Doctors still have a great hold on our belief system, even though their knowledge comes primarily from only one perspective: that of Western medicine. I think it is a mistake for doctors to give someone a death sentence; they know too little to make such predictions, and because of the status we accord doctors, our thought processes regularly fulfill their prophecies.

I believe that many of us need a serious motivation before we will re-examine our lives and do some literal soul-searching. A death sentence can fill that role if it doesn't completely cripple us. But it's sad to see people buy into it completely, unable to see all their options. Disease comes into our lives for many different reasons, and only through self-examination can we find our own personal truth. It takes in-depth honesty, wisdom, and knowledge to direct the experience of a particular lifetime. Never let your own soul's power bend before the perceptions of someone else, for you don't know where they are on their own evolutionary journey. Do what truly feels right for you.

Ellen had heard about the success of Pat's healing and decided it was something she wanted to try. I did a meditation and tuned in to Ellen as part of the process of deciding whether I thought the healing could help her. I hadn't met her yet and I was trying to get a sense of the situation. I got quite a positive feeling. I wasn't as energized as I had been when I tuned in to Pat, but it felt as if the healing had potential. I also sensed that Ellen was very busy, always on the go, mostly for other people. I felt she needed to slow down and be still in mind and body for a while.

Ellen came for the healing and we booked a two-week period for her. She was lovely and beautiful, a gentle spirit. She was open and did not seem at all self-conscious about giving herself fully to the healings. She was also very thin and found it hard to eat. She was on a fairly high dose of morphine; because the doctors felt she would not live to come off it, they believed the dosage didn't matter.

We had two sessions of healing a day. They went very well. One day I saw an image of the tumour. It looked like a corkscrew. I thought I must be wrong—I was sure tumours didn't look like that—so I was uneasy about mentioning it to

Ellen. Seeing something like this was a new experience for me, and because it didn't look the way I thought it should, I was skeptical. It was myself, as usual, that I doubted.

But I did mention it, and to my surprise Ellen told me that her tumour did look like a corkscrew, just as I described. I was so pleased that I had taken the risk of telling her because it showed me I was getting information accurately. This was a big step for me, and I was grateful that I was becoming more sensitive to detail.

Very soon, Ellen began to get her appetite back and was able to slowly reduce her morphine. I could see her improving every day, and it was really exciting. She just looked so much more alive.

We had many insightful visions during the healings. In one of them, Ellen's mom, who had passed away a few years earlier, made an appearance. She gave me enough information for Ellen to know it was her mother. Messages from the spirit world during healings can be healing in themselves. Just knowing you have the love and support of departed loved ones is very uplifting. But I find that contact with those in Spirit energy also raises my own frequency and energizes me with a feeling of immense joy and love.

A few months after Ellen returned home, she had an MRI. Her doctor was amazed to find that the tumour was shrinking. He asked her how she thought such an unexpected turnaround in her health could be possible. She credited an improved diet and energy healing.

Ellen very quickly became busy again. She phoned me one day to say she had just returned from Mexico. She asked me how going away could be wrong when it brought her such happiness to dance on the beach with her grandchildren. I said that it sounded lovely, but I wondered if Ellen was taking time for herself. Then she and her husband were off to Turkey on a tour. I could tell that Ellen was concerned about going on this trip and the lack of control she would have because it was a tour. She asked me if I thought she should go, and I told her she would have to do what she wanted. She also had a reading with a medium and asked if she would have a relapse with the cancer on the trip, but the medium could not see that happening. So Ellen decided to go.

I think she felt pressure to be amazing and upbeat, to be a good sport, and to surprise people with how well she was doing. She had a constant desire to please, to be the one everyone could count on to be there, to never let anyone down. And that's a wonderful kind of person to be. But as I'm learning myself, slowly, there has to be a balance. I think Ellen felt inside that she shouldn't go. I believe, in retrospect, that Ellen wanted me to tell her not to go. At the time, I didn't have that insight and felt it wasn't my place to tell her how to live her life.

I'm not criticizing Ellen. I see a lot of myself in her. Sometimes I go, go, go, so busy rushing around that I don't take time to connect to my soul. For all of us, there is something in this lifetime that we wanted to remember when we came back to the physical plane, a connection to Source to remind us what we are really meant to be while we live this life. When I slow down, connecting with my inner self, my perception and insight into my life take on a completely different level of meaning and understanding. It is critical that we make this connection because it is the core of who we are and why this life matters. In Ellen, I saw someone who needed to slow down and get in touch with her soul.

Occasionally someone will tell me a story that says so much more than the words themselves. Ellen told me about a time when she was riding in a car with her husband and his ex-wife, who were talking about the extreme sports and physical activities they loved to do. They asked her what she wanted to try. She felt self-conscious and lacking, because the thing she was really excited about was delving into a new cookbook she had recently bought. She wanted to study the recipes and start trying them. As she was telling me the story, it seemed that she felt she was less than, an underachiever, because her passion was so passive. It wasn't a big adventure or feat of endurance. But cooking can be a very creative act, and when done with inspiration, it can provide a wonderful connection to your inner self. Nevertheless, Ellen felt apologetic for her mild ways. This story told me of Ellen's yearning for balance, her need to slow down, but her desire to please others took precedence.

I talked to her and her husband about taking it easy for a while after the healing sessions. I suggested they might walk through the aspen trees on their beautiful property, sit in their hot tub, and lie in the grass in the sun. They held hands and were quite emotional about taking time to just be. They listened, but I'm not sure they heard what I was saying.

Ellen had been having a problem with gallstones for some time, but couldn't have her gallbladder removed because the cancerous tumour was so close to it. But now that her tumour was shrinking and it was small enough to allow them to remove her gallbladder safely, her doctor had finally scheduled the surgery. It wasn't a difficult operation and she needed it, but she decided not to have the surgery so she could go on holiday with her family.

A few months later, Ellen went on the trip to Turkey. When she returned, she discovered she had contracted a severe parasite—one, it seems, the doctors couldn't figure out how to treat. She grew weaker and weaker. She appeared to lose her will to take control and her strength to try. Then her gallbladder, full of stones, backed up and bile filled her stomach. Ellen phoned me from the hospital. She was vomiting bile.

At the time, all I could think of was that I had let her down. If I had tried harder, she would have been okay. I felt that I must have disappointed her. I couldn't think of wise words to say over the phone, and I felt I couldn't help with the healing at this point. Jeff and I made the trip to Alberta to see her at her home. She was frail and weak, and realized that she didn't have long to live. I tried to do a healing with her, but it felt like I wasn't really helping. It was as if a corner had been turned, decisions had been made, and a new direction was being taken.

A few weeks later, she passed away. I was devastated, and could not come to terms with what had happened. Did it have to end this way? Was it meant to be? Was Ellen's death inevitable? Was it simply her time to pass? Or do we live moment to moment, making our choices, the consequences unfolding before us, the outcomes open to all possibilities?

I feel that we come into this life with a plan, but we have free will to decide what to do in our day-to-day life. If we take time to connect to our inner self, our soul, maybe we'll be still long enough to sense the pull of our soul's desire, know the direction we're meant to go, and make the choices we planned for ourselves before we came into this lifetime.

I don't know what Ellen's plan was and I wasn't here to decide for her, but I felt Ellen wanted to live. She talked of writing books and teaching people about her spiritual journey. When she hugged me goodbye after the healings, she didn't want to let go. She loved the healings, where she and I connected, soul to soul. When things had seemed so right in the healing, why did they have to go so wrong? I felt incredibly discouraged about continuing my journey as a healer.

But it was important for me to remember that, from the perspective of the spirit world, life is just a fleeting glance and death is not an end. Life is an opportunity to learn, to experience, to let go when the time is right. I thank you, Ellen, for sharing your experience and love with me.

LEARNING TO TRUST

Chelsea

FELT SUCH SADNESS and loss at Ellen's passing, and no matter what wise thoughts I tried to impart to myself, I didn't seem to listen. I couldn't help wondering if I could have done more. Disillusioned with the healing and questioning my ability to help people, I simply didn't want to be part of something that left me feeling responsible for someone's death. I desperately needed to move on. As it was, it was time to move to England and start editing the film about Charlie and the grizzlies in Russia. It was a relief to go back to my old lifestyle.

This was going to be an incredible film. We had an opportunity to share Charlie's understanding and experiences of grizzly bears and show their true nature. I was full of ideas of how it should be presented. Jeff had captured on film very profound moments with Charlie and the bears. Because Charlie had lived with the bears, he had unique insights into their behaviour, as well as into the great range of emotions they experience and their strong sensitivity to the emotional energy given off by others, both bears and people. What excited me was that he had found how powerful the energy of emotion is, and that it can be felt and reflected without physical or verbal communication. If a person was experiencing fear or anger but was in no way acting outwardly on those feelings, the bear would still respond with fear or aggression. But if the person was feeling love and respect for the bear, the bear would respond by being calm and relaxed. The film was a fantastic example of the physical effect that the frequency of emotional energy has on both people and animals. Thankfully, Charlie was comfortable enough with himself to tell the truth as he experienced it.

The main message of the film is that bears are complex, intelligent, sensitive creatures who deserve to be treated with dignity and respect. If we can try to understand that their responses to us very much mirror our attitudes towards them, then it shouldn't be a big jump for us to learn how to live peacefully as their neighbours. I was passionate about this exciting and remarkable project, and eager to get to work.

We had rented a lovely old house in Bristol, the biggest we had ever stayed in while editing in England. Three storeys high, it had a huge kitchen, big windows, a lovely sitting room, and—best of all for a mom—a large laundry room, a rarity in England. In most of our previous homes in England there had been a combo washer-dryer tucked into a kitchen cupboard space, if we were lucky. And this home also had a wonderful, private back garden.

Of course, Jeff and I got first dibs on our bedroom, and then Chelsea and Logan excitedly explored our new home, deciding which of the four bedrooms they would claim as their own. Logan, then eleven years old, chose a cozy attic room. Gazing down to the street below, you felt as though you were in a secret hideaway, higher than everyone else in the neighbourhood. The ceiling, all different angles and shapes, could have been right out of Hogwarts. Chelsea, who was now fourteen, chose a lovely room on its own floor with a large window that looked over the back garden. It was very peaceful. But what drew Chelsea to it were the many bookshelves filled with classic old books. The room could have belonged to Jane Austen. Both my children were happily settled, and this made me happy as well.

We soon adjusted to our new routine. Jeff worked fulltime at the BBC while I split my day between helping the kids with their school work in the morning and editing in the afternoon. Living in a city presented Chelsea and Logan with opportunities very different from their country life in Canada. Chelsea, keen to volunteer at a charity shop, applied at a few close to the BBC. She soon got a part-time job at a little shop that sold clothing and knick-knacks to raise money for St. Peter's Hospice, where Hazel had spent the last few days of her life.

Our life in England was going well. Logan became good friends with a boy who lived close by and they were always getting together to play after school. Chelsea joined a theatre school, which she loved, and was making friends with kids her age. But after a month or so, she began experiencing unsettling symptoms: her heart would start to race, her chest felt tight, and she had difficulty breathing and weakness all over. At first I thought she was having panic attacks brought on by anxiety. But Chelsea said she wasn't feeling stressed, other than being worried about what was going on with her body. We were very close and we talked a lot, but we couldn't determine what was causing these symptoms.

Soon, things started to escalate. Chelsea became nauseous and vomited whatever she ate. We tried changing her diet, but her body did not seem able to tolerate anything. I searched desperately for help in every place I could think of, taking her for acupuncture and consulting homeopathic and naturopathic doctors.

Chelsea was getting weaker by the day. She was losing a lot of weight and was light-headed. One day, when we were in London staying at a hotel, Chelsea became very sick. Her heartbeat was irregular and she couldn't stand up. We called emergency and a doctor came to our hotel. After examining Chelsea, she told us to get her to the emergency department at the hospital. There, they did an electrocardiogram and all sorts of other tests, but they couldn't determine the cause of her sickness.

We went back to Bristol and I stayed by Chelsea's side. I held her beside me for hours, wrapped in quilts to keep her warm. I fed her small amounts of soup or Jell-O, but she could tolerate only a couple of teaspoons.

I never thought of trying to heal her. In my mind, I had left healing behind. After Ellen's death, I had unequivocally decided my healing wasn't very powerful, and I had no intention of wasting time on something that wasn't going to help Chelsea. She needed real help from professionals.

Now very thin and weak, Chelsea vomited and had diarrhea whenever she ate anything. She was filled with fear. When she continued to have problems with her heart and breathing, we rushed her into the emergency department at the Bristol hospital. Again, a series of tests was carried out on her heart and the rest of her body, but they couldn't figure out what was causing all of these symptoms.

As I sat with Chelsea one day, I felt complete panic and knew for certain that we had reached a crisis. Chelsea's life was at risk if we didn't get help right now. I went to my bedroom and meditated for answers. I prayed for help. The message I got, in no uncertain terms, was to get to work healing Chelsea. It was like someone saying, "For God's sake, what are you waiting for? Do a healing with her now."

I grabbed blankets and ran down the stairs. I cleared off the kitchen table and spread the blankets across it. I closed the curtains. I helped Chelsea onto the table. As I did the healing, my hands worked very fast, creating patterns of movement all over her. I don't remember much else about the healing or how long it lasted.

Chelsea started to feel better almost immediately. In a few hours she began to eat, and at dinnertime she ate a full meal. This was after weeks of seeing her ingest only a few spoonfuls. The nausea and diarrhea stopped, and Chelsea's fear was gone. The next day she had the strength to write an exam for school and go over to a friend's house. The immediacy of her recovery was astounding. It took her a while to regain her weight and muscle strength, but it was clear she was on the mend.

We had been in England for nearly four months by this time, and I was relieved to be returning to Canada. When we got home, I took Chelsea to our naturopathic doctor for a checkup and to get some supplements to boost her immune system. I told him that I had begun to wonder whether Chelsea's problems in England had started with mould. Perhaps she had come into contact with mould when sorting clothes in the charity shop basement or touching the old books in her bedroom. He tested her lungs and found that she did have indicators for mould. He explained to me that once one system in the body becomes compromised, the rest are vulnerable, a domino effect. When Chelsea's respiratory system was weakened, her digestive system, nervous system, and circulatory system also failed.

I also took Chelsea to our regular doctor, who said that she showed signs of infection in her chest and that she would have to be very careful until she had completely recovered. Both doctors were quite alarmed at how sick Chelsea was, but Jeff and I knew she was a hundred times better than she had been in England.

When I prayed for help for Chelsea and was told to do a healing on her, I vowed that if it helped her, I would stay true to the healing process in the future and honour it in any way I could. In desperation, I had asked for a miracle; to my relief, I was granted one. I wanted to show my deepest respect for this incredible healing, but I also realized that doing so might expose me to more healings like Ellen's, which had left me feeling devastated. Regardless, I renewed my commitment to Spirit and to Source energy to continue on my healing path, although I had no idea what this really meant for me.

ON YOUR PROGRAM

Giorgio

M Y DEAR FRIEND Charlie called me from the film festival in Telluride, Colorado. Our film about him and the grizzlies in Russia, *The Edge of Eden*, had won the Best of Festival award. We were unable to attend the festival, but Charlie had gone.

"I met this man," Charlie said, his voice steady. "He's just had brain surgery and I think you could help him. He's a really neat guy and I think he would be open to it. They think he hasn't much time to live."

"I don't know, Charlie," I said. "I don't know if I can do it." I still felt insecure about doing healings. Although I had not forgotten the commitment I had made only months before to honour the healing energy, this sounded like a rather serious healing for me to be starting on again. "Does he have any other options? Charlie . . . did you already tell him about me?"

"Yes, well, a little, but I didn't give him your number. But would it be all right if I did?"

"Yes," I said, hesitantly.

Charlie always believed in me more than I believed in myself. He joked that he was my agent. Forthright and seemingly unable to contain himself, he just had to mention the healing to people. And that's exactly what I needed, to be put out there to strangers, because I was too reserved to do it myself. But I needed to start learning all I could about healing, and for that I needed patients.

Giorgio did not call for a few weeks. Then, one day, there he was on the end of the line. He and his partner, Arlene, both wanted to learn more about what I did.

Giorgio had had a tumour removed from his brain, but another was forming. He was losing the use of his left arm and was having trouble walking.

I heard myself saying, "I have no medical background or education in healing. I don't know if I can help you at all, or what I would even do to try to help. I have never done anything like this before. Have you carefully considered all your other options?"

But I also talked about my experiences so far and my feelings about healing. I could tell that Giorgio connected to my honesty and to what I was saying about the energy and how I thought it worked.

He was in. He wanted to get together but was too sick to travel to Canada. Arlene and Giorgio were staying in a beach house just outside San Francisco. Because I could be close to nature and walk on the beach, I thought I would be able to work there. I was intrigued by the challenge. It would be a huge test of the power of the energy and of what was possible.

Chelsea agreed to travel with me; I definitely would not have gone alone. I needed someone I could count on for support, someone I could trust 100 percent, who knew me so well that she could help keep me centred and grounded. Chelsea is one of the very few people able to fill that role.

We packed and flew to San Francisco, arriving on July 1. That I would fly from home to stay with people I knew almost nothing about showed how strong a pull my soul's desire had on me. Once I had made the decision to help Giorgio, I felt that this was what I was meant to do. We know we're on our path when it feels so right.

I didn't really know what to expect, but I had ideas about diet, meditations, and things we should talk about. It was a huge step for me, that's for sure.

Chelsea and I took a bus from the airport to Stinson Beach, north of San Francisco. We got off the bus and were met by a lovely Italian man, a friend of Giorgio's just over from Italy for a visit. He spoke little English. We drove through the mountains to come back down to the ocean. At this point I had to trust and believe that what we were doing was safe and that Chelsea and I would be okay.

We came to a beautiful little white house on a long stretch of beach. The sound of the waves and the wind gave me a great sense of peace. I looked forward to long walks with Chelsea and the freedom and privacy this place would offer us.

Arlene welcomed us and took me right into the bedroom to meet Giorgio. He was very weak and seemed to find it hard to open his eyes. I could tell he had little energy for words. I sat on the bed. We said a few simple things, and I introduced myself and tried to get a sense of him. I'm not certain he knew for sure who I was. We talked briefly, but I didn't really feel he was up for thinking about what I was saying. He looked only partly there; in his lovely brown eyes he seemed very far away, and I knew I couldn't reach him with words. He had virtually nothing left. He couldn't sit up or get out of bed on his own. He wasn't eating or drinking much of anything. The fresh fruit drink we fixed for him made him vomit.

Giorgio's hair, which had been shaved for his last operation, was just starting to grow back, and I could see the large scar across his head, arcing around half of his skull. I knew that, hidden somewhere in his tired, sick body, there was a person I would like to know, but in his frail condition it was hard to make any connection.

We had to lift Giorgio onto the healing table at the end of the bed for me to do the healings. It was quite a feat. Arlene was strong and athletic, and understood how to work with Giorgio's body to get him where we needed him.

Then, in the privacy and quiet of the bedroom, I tried to get into a relaxed and calm place. It felt right to work only on his head. That first day, my hands began to pat and circle, doing all kinds of energy work. I never understood exactly why I was working on a particular spot or if I was making any progress. I had to keep my mind out of the process and I had to trust.

The next day, we got Giorgio back on the healing table. He always seemed to have a headache, so it made me quite self-conscious to be working on his head. But minutes after I started the healing, he would go into a deep sleep. I think this was better for him and for me. While I was working, the only image I saw in my mind was a turtle. I didn't know what this meant. Maybe it was to show me we were moving slowly, and that moving slowly was okay.

I had planned to do two healings each day. Giorgio slept almost all day except for about thirty minutes. He liked to sit up for a few minutes and have a cigarette or a few sips of coffee. I didn't get the impression he was naturally a smoker, but I think these things gave him a tiny sense of peace. He wasn't interested in eating or drinking juices. It felt as if we had hardly anything going for us. He was no longer interested in nutrition, and I couldn't talk to him about energy or my feelings about what I thought he should do to get better—he was too tired and weak to care.

I was starting to feel very unsure about the healing and myself. I didn't know where he was at. We felt so separate. Arlene and I managed to get him on the healing table again. When she left us, Giorgio almost immediately fell asleep. But then, as I was about to start the healing, Giorgio opened his eyes and looked up into mine. He very quietly said, "I'm on your program. You may not know it, but I'm on your program." This was a huge moment for me. It gave me an enormous boost. Giorgio and I had connected and I wasn't alone on this healing journey. He couldn't have given me a better gift. Then he went off into a deep sleep. He slept through the healing and for a few hours after. Then we put him back in bed and he went to sleep again. Arlene told me that with this type of cancer, people just sleep more and more until one time they don't wake up. I had been picturing the sleeping as healing time, but now I felt really rocked on my foundation: maybe he was just descending into death.

I walked for miles along the beach. I sat on the sand and looked out at the ocean and asked why. Why had I been brought here? Giorgio was close to death. Arlene told me that the doctor had said on the Friday before I arrived that if Giorgio didn't have another surgery on Monday, he wouldn't last the week. I had arrived on Sunday. I knew that Giorgio did not want surgery and that I was his last port of call.

So why was I here? I didn't feel I was doing much. Was I brought here to experience death? Did my guides, my Spirit energy, want me to witness someone dying? Was that what this whole trip was for? And what about Chelsea? Giorgio's death would be hard on her. I was so confused, and now, as I thought about it, all I felt was scared. The trip wasn't at all what I had thought it would be. The ocean and sand were my saving grace; I needed to stay close to nature. I was beyond grateful for Chelsea's company.

On the morning of my third full day of healing, I saw an image of a cheetah. I wasn't sure what that meant—was the healing moving faster? It didn't seem to be. When I finished the healing with my hands, I got down on my knees at the head of the healing table and blew energy through my heart chakra straight into the top of Giorgio's head. I was hoping maybe this would do something more, something more powerful. I do not know if Spirit was guiding me or if it was a spontaneous decision, but it felt right.

After the healing, Chelsea and I decided to go down to the beach. Arlene put Giorgio in his wheelchair so he could sit outside for a little while. He was with Eleonora, his ex-wife, and Tom, the neighbour. As I went by them, I could hear Tom saying to Giorgio that he must have the operation. There was so much fear in the air. Giorgio looked to be in his last few days. Maybe he should rush to Italy and have another operation. I wanted to believe in the healing, but maybe Giorgio was too far gone, maybe it was too late.

As I was coming back from the beach, Tom and Eleonora were having a serious talk with Arlene. They wanted to get a private jet to fly Giorgio to Italy. I decided to go back to the beach. I was sure I knew what they thought about the healing, and my confidence was very low. I wondered if Chelsea and I should fly back to Canada early. I felt very out of place. I phoned Jeff on my cellphone from the beach and I know I sounded very tired. I sat and watched the waves until I had the strength to return.

As I came back up to the house, Arlene was running to meet me. Giorgio was asking for another healing. She was very excited, because he had moved his left arm, and his left leg and arm were getting warm. I came in and did the healing. Giorgio went into a peaceful sleep. He seemed to be unaware of me. I felt desperate to try harder. I sat in a chair facing the end of the healing table, at Giorgio's head. I decided to put my forehead on Giorgio's forehead, and then I brought energy down through my crown chakra and out through my forehead into his. Again and again, I felt the energy flow through me. I opened myself up. I could not be self-conscious—I had to work from my soul, as honest and true as I could be. Giorgio's mind, I was sure, was unaware as he slept, so it couldn't get in the way of the healing. It was a spontaneous action, but it felt quite powerful.

By the next day, Giorgio could sit up well enough that he wanted me to take him for a walk in his wheelchair. I walked for about an hour, pushing him. We were two people who knew hardly a thing about each other, brought together at a critical moment. We were doing something so intimate, the transferring of life-giving energy at the eleventh hour, but on a personal level I felt unsure of how to talk to Giorgio. Everything I thought to say felt so frivolous. He talked to me about Italy, cars, and flying airplanes. As he talked, I was getting to know him a little. Giorgio was still in there.

On the afternoon of our fifth day, I saw Giorgio sitting in his wheelchair outside in the sunshine. Later, when he came into the living room, we had music playing. I went over to him and his wheelchair and took his hands to dance. As I looked down at Giorgio, he was softly crying. He had loved to dance when he was well, and he was deeply moved by the music. I knelt in front of him and looked deep into his eyes. And then, for a few moments, I felt this incredible connection. I had travelled, it felt, right through to his soul, in a way that is hard to describe in words, because it was otherworldly. I wasn't seeing the person of this lifetime; I was seeing through to his eternal soul. I knew he was now well enough to start making a huge emotional shift.

Eleonora had told me a few days before about Giorgio describing for her one time what he was like as a boy of seven. He would look in the mirror and decide how he wanted his face to look, the shape of his nose and eyebrows. In time, he was able to create the face he wanted. I knew this was the link I needed to get him to connect to the power of his soul, to get him to remember. I knew; he knew. He had the power. He had the connection with this incredible energy to transform his body. He knew that if he could do it as a child with his face, he could do it now with his healing.

Giorgio sat there crying and saying, "I remember, I remember." He looked into my eyes and said, "We have done this together."

That night, Giorgio sat at the table and ate dinner with us and told stories of his childhood. One of his earliest memories was when his little sister, Marina, was born. His father took him to the nursery to see all the babies and pick out the one he wanted. They looked them over, one by one. With some subtle suggestions from his dad, each baby they looked at was not quite right—too big a nose, odd-shaped ears, wrong hair—until they finally got to his sister, who was unknown to Giorgio. They looked her over and decided she was just right, so they agreed they would take her home. Giorgio said he could never complain about her crying or behaviour because his father was quick to remind him that he was the one who had picked her out.

Giorgio's mind, eyes, and voice were clear. After dinner, I did a healing on his head as he sat in his wheelchair in the bedroom. He told me how grateful he was to everyone. He thanked me and held my hand. I said good night, and as I was leaving the room, he told me to sleep well and that he would send me good thoughts in the night.

I was getting to know Giorgio. He was emotionally and mentally back, as if he had turned a corner. Now we needed more healing in his body.

The next day, Giorgio had a really good appetite and wanted a smoothie for breakfast.

He sat out in the sunshine and ate his lunch and didn't want to take a nap. I was starting to see his sense of humour. He said that if his hair started to turn blond and curl, the hand patting on his head in the healings was getting too strong.

As the days passed, everyone's spirits were rising. There was laughter, music playing, and food being prepared in the kitchen. Giorgio could feel the love from everyone around him and from the healing source of the universe. He was being filled to the brim with love energy.

One day he said he had never felt so much love. He felt like getting down on his knees and giving thanks. At a wonderful moment, Giorgio said to me, "Do I look ridiculously happy for the shape I'm in?" And although he was in a wheelchair and could do little on his own, the high-vibrational energy was so intense that joy radiated around us.

I was starting to get some insights into Giorgio as a person. He had a wonderful sense of humour. He was kind and gentle, loved espresso and Italian cheese, loved adventure and being active, loved music, loved nature, loved being free. He felt things deeply, and experiences he had with people in his life affected him profoundly. Giorgio had many friends, but I found him to be a very private person. In time we shared meaningful conversations and I started to understand his journey.

Giorgio was only partway along his route to healing when the time came for Chelsea and me to go home. We had arranged to stay a week. I felt very tired. I had used myself up physically and emotionally, and needed to get home. So much had happened in a week—Chelsea and I had arrived to meet strangers and now were saying goodbye to friends.

We had been back home only ten days when Arlene and Giorgio called me to say that Giorgio was now able to stand and take a step with someone supporting him. It was very exciting—his body was starting to work again. Giorgio was so keen on the healing that he wanted me to return. So Chelsea and I were off again, arriving in San Francisco on July 21 feeling pumped. My confidence grew.

The next day, Giorgio took his first steps on the beach. It was incredible to see. He could also lift his left arm. On Tuesday, we had an amazing healing. During it, Giorgio started moving the fingers of his left hand. When I finished the healing, he opened his eyes and said, "Wow." He said he could feel the energy coming into his head like a stream of high-powered water, and that he could then tune in to the energy and adjust it where it needed to go, like being in a shower.

Giorgio had a degree in nuclear engineering. I liked his very scientific mind. I wanted to work with someone who could see the healing for the incredible energy it was and that, though it was beyond our comprehension in many ways, it was still real and tangible. Giorgio, who could easily combine the wisdom of science and the spiritual into one world, had the vision to understand the higher frequencies of energy. He had an independent mind and didn't need to conform to society's sometimes limited vision. This free-spirited quality manifested in the lifestyle he had created, combining his love of nature and travel. He owned his own plane and a private flying company that did adventure tours in North and South America. He flew tour groups to Alaska or remote locations in South America, offering people the chance to visit unique and private destinations that the mainstream travel companies could not service. He also cared deeply about the Earth and its animals, and was passionate about life. His perspective, derived from both his education and his experiences, made his appreciation and respect for the healing very meaningful to me.

The whole left side of Giorgio's body started coming back. Everyone was so thrilled, full of love and joy, cocooning him in a safe and nurturing environment. Giorgio's mom and sister arrived from Italy; friends came to visit. On Thursday, July 26, Giorgio walked down the beach with a walking stick; on the 27th, he walked without the stick. On the 29th, Giorgio ran on the beach. It was so much to take in, to try to comprehend.

Giorgio's mom and I watched through the window as he walked beside the ocean. I sat with my arms around her as she softly cried and spoke to me in Italian. Although we couldn't speak the same language, the language of love is universal—it's a sensation, not words.

Giorgio and I went for a morning run on the beach. I couldn't have been more happy or grateful. But the meaning and the implications behind what we had witnessed were so profound, it was impossible to truly get my head around them. From my point of view, what I had to offer this healing energy was myself—being an open, loving, compassionate person. But I could only go with the energy, respecting it, appreciating it, understanding that it was still very much a mystery to me.

On the afternoon of the 29th, Chelsea and I flew home. I had done thirty-two healings with Giorgio in July. When I had arrived on July 1, he couldn't move around by himself and could barely talk, eat, or drink; he slept twenty-two or twenty-three hours a day. Now, four weeks later, he was running on the beach.

When I think of this, I always need to stop and let it sink in. There is a huge message for all humans in this experience. We have available to us an energy that is far beyond our imagination, and it seems to have limitless possibilities. What we need to bring to the equation is love, gratitude, and trust. That's what I understand so far.

Giorgio had another MRI on August 13. The surgeon said the tumour was gone and things couldn't look better. Giorgio said he wanted to run and dance around the doctor's desk, shouting, "Look at me now, I feel incredible. The tumour is gone because of energy healing." But because I had asked him to keep secret the fact that I did energy healing, he disappointedly said nothing.

The family and friends, the love, the healings, and Giorgio's passion and determination were the perfect recipe for recovery and wellness.

Shortly after Chelsea and I returned home, Giorgio's mother and sister went back to Italy. Then, a few weeks later, Giorgio was told that he would have to move out of his friend's beach house. After months of paying huge medical bills for the removal of his first tumour and two subsequent surgeries to deal with complications, money was a huge source of stress. Now, having to move, he had no security or plan of what to do. Giorgio had gone from being surrounded by the highest levels of vibration, the energy of joy, love, and gratitude, to being overtaken by the lowest levels of vibration, the energy of fear, powerlessness, insecurity, and despair.

Giorgio, Arlene, and her good friend Craig decided to drive north to visit me in British Columbia. On their way, they stopped in Oregon for Arlene's sister's wedding. Giorgio was starting to feel unwell again and experienced a small seizure, indicating that a third tumour was growing.

It was a long trip. Giorgio would call me from the road, anxious because he was starting to lose control of his left side again. I would send him distance healing and meditate, trying to find answers. When they were within a day of the border, Giorgio lost the use of his left hand and arm and was having trouble walking without help. The tumour was growing quickly.

I decided to meet them at a motel on the Canadian side of the border. It felt as if we couldn't start healing fast enough.

Giorgio walked down the hallway of the motel, Craig on one side and Arlene on the other. It seemed impossible that we could have lost so much ground so quickly. I had Giorgio lie on the bed with his head at the foot so I could sit in a chair and work on his head. During this first short healing, he started to move the fingers of his left hand again. He was so excited and happy.

The next day, we drove to my place. I could see that Giorgio was greatly relieved to have arrived. The healing started to help quite quickly. On the second day Giorgio was at our house, I drove him up the mountain to find a quiet place in nature where he could meditate. He could hardly stand up, so I helped him out of the truck and then pivoted his body to sit in a chair right beside it. When I took him back up the mountain only two days later, he could walk alone—over sticks and around rocks—to a chair twenty-five feet from the truck.

The next day, Giorgio started to get very upsetting e-mails from Italy, from the mother of his young son. She was cutting him off from his son and Giorgio wouldn't be able to see him again. Giorgio cared deeply about his son. He and the boy's mother had very different values, and he worried about how his son was being raised. Then he received more e-mails from friends with upsetting news. Giorgio was angry and disappointed in some of the people he had thought were his friends. People he had been sure he could count on were now letting him down. And he was feeling desperate about the future because he and Arlene did not have a plan.

One night, as Giorgio and I sat in the living room, he anxiously told me that he could feel a seizure coming on in his head. I had been scared of something like this happening, because from our remote home it was a four-hour drive to a hospital that could help him. I sat by his side and did a healing on his head. As my hands moved, the seizure stopped. It was surreal, a miracle in itself. Then Giorgio got up, walked quietly to the kitchen, sat down, and ate dinner. Something beyond our comprehension had just happened: a few movements of my hands and some flowing energy had stopped the seizure. How was it possible? Even with all that was wrong, the healing energy still flowed through. The universe and Spirit sent their unconditional love, no matter what.

Stress and anger flooded back into Giorgio's life. One day he told me that throughout the whole healing we'd just done, he had been arguing in his mind with his son's mother. In hindsight, we should have turned off the computers and phones to protect him from those who would purposely inflict pain. There was no longer a clear passage through to Giorgio. The lines were filled with messages that would become life-threatening. We needed a safe healing environment with no pressure of time or outside intrusions. But I was unable to provide that place. Jeff was away filming. Chelsea and Logan were doing school by correspondence and I was their teacher. I was completely overwhelmed. I wanted to focus on the healing, but by the time I had sorted out everything else, I had very little energy left.

I needed a healing centre and a guest house. I was doing healings either in my bathroom or outside. Giorgio and Arlene were sleeping in our living room. None of us had space or privacy. I was learning as I was going, and I did not have the resources to do anything differently.

One day, Giorgio and I were sitting on the edge of his bed in the living room. The washing machine had just broken down, and we could not function without it for even a day; with so many in the house, laundry piled up quickly. I had to drive thirty kilometres into town immediately to buy a new machine. Giorgio wanted to pay for it, but I didn't let him. He said that one day, in some way, he was going to help me.

Despite the challenges we were facing, Giorgio and I shared a lot of laughs. Giorgio had not been raised around animals. At our home, chickens, ducks, a peacock, dogs, and cats all run loose in the garden. One morning Giorgio was sitting outside eating his breakfast when a chicken came up and stole his toast right out of his hand. The peacock then chased the chicken and stole the toast from her, all to Giorgio's amusement and disbelief.

We were raising two ducklings by hand after finding their eggs in the garden, abandoned by their mother. These two babes loved to be with people and would cuddle on Giorgio's chest as he lay in bed. They gave him great joy and delight, and probably brought through a lot of healing energy.

I believe that, if we could have sorted out his living situation and brought him peace of mind about the future, the healing would have been successful. Unfortunately, Giorgio's life circumstances kept worsening.

One day, Giorgio and Arlene went to town so that he could walk on paved roads. Something upset him and he became desperately depressed. Arlene told me that he banged his head on the car, saying he wanted to die. Giorgio was a private person and I never liked to push people, so I did not ask him what had happened. Maybe I should have. It seemed like a turning point in the wrong direction.

Nevertheless, we continued the healing treatments. Giorgio felt they were really helping and wanted to stay longer than they had planned; it seemed of the utmost importance to him. But for reasons I'm not sure of now, we took only a few extra days, when what we needed was weeks of calm, without interruptions. The day before Giorgio and Arlene were to leave, he told me he was going to hide and that when their car drove away, he wouldn't be in it, and that I would hear him calling, "Susan, Susan, Susan," from the bushes.

But Giorgio did not hide in the bushes. It was heartbreaking to see them drive away. It felt like the beginning of the end.

Giorgio's trip to Canada had been an adventure, and our worlds had met on common ground, one of love and compassion. I have often thought since then how culture, country, and tradition have nothing to do with healing. We all heal the same way; we all need the same things to be well. Our souls are all made of the same stuff: love. Italian man from the city or Canadian gal from the country—it makes no difference.

Within days of leaving, Giorgio and Arlene made the difficult journey back to Italy, returning to his childhood home, mother, sister, and lifelong friends. Doctors operated, but in trying to cut out the third tumour, they cut out some of his brain. Giorgio lost most of the movement in his body and was virtually blind.

Jeff and I went to Italy to see him. Jeff had never met him, and I wanted to see if there was anything I could do to help. Giorgio said he did not want to live if most of his eyesight was gone. So the trip became more a reunion and goodbye than a healing. I had such a strong connection to Giorgio's spirit that getting to know his world was a gift.

Giorgio maintained his great sense of humour, and now that he was in the sanctuary of his family home and country, a sense of peace had come back to him. Giorgio's sister Marina felt the healing had greatly helped him to be in the highest form of energy for the journey through death, coming out of this lifetime already connected to his soul and ready to move on to higher levels of being.

When Giorgio died, I felt confused and sad, as if part of me had died with him. He and I had been partners in understanding ourselves as energetic beings, a great link in the chain. He had been so easy to work with. I was sure he was a piece of the puzzle, now gone. I believed I had failed: I had failed Giorgio, I had failed myself, I had failed the world.

I was almost certain that I had to give up on this path. It was too painful. I believed, without a doubt, that there is a Universal energy that is the lifeblood of all that is, that we all have connections to this energy and to a spiritual energy realm, and that raising our own vibrational energy to heal ourselves and heal others is only the beginning of what is possible. But now I felt I was not the person to help bring forth this story. I had thought I could, but I couldn't. I didn't have it in me. My regular life was so much simpler and more enjoyable, so much less challenging.

It didn't occur to me at the time that the surgeon who had removed Giorgio's first tumour probably didn't feel that he had failed because a second one grew. In the month that I first did healings on him, Giorgio's second tumour shrank away and he went from being in a virtual coma to running on the beach. I had almost completely lost sight of the miraculous healing we had all witnessed. But we did not remove the causes of the cancer from Giorgio's being, so although we were able to get rid of the second tumour, just as the surgeon had been able to get rid of the first one, the underlying conditions for tumour growth remained. I believe that those conditions were deep anger and sadness, an acidic diet with quite a bit of dairy, and a feeling of loss of control in his life.

After Giorgio died, all of this was a blur to me. I piled guilt upon myself for what I could have done to save his life, and I felt very sad for Arlene and his family. I also grieved the loss of Giorgio personally, because it seemed he was someone I could have worked with. Keen and intrigued by the way the healing energy worked, Giorgio had said he would help me to learn all I could. He even thought I might be able to meet a scientist he knew in South America who could measure energy waves and photograph Spirit and energy patterns. But now Giorgio was gone.

I lost my enthusiasm for my life when I stopped exploring this incredible understanding of energy and my deep-rooted belief that human appreciation of this energy's potential could change our relationship to the Earth. My experiences with Spirit energy and Universal or Divine energy had completely changed my perspective on living. The light of my soul had shone so brightly when my feet were firmly on my path. But now my spirit flipped around and I felt dark inside. In my outer world, I still had all the things I loved most. Jeff, Chelsea, and Logan stood by my side and never faltered in their admiration for all that we had witnessed in the healings in the past years, and they never stopped believing that it wasn't over. They patiently waited for the winds of change to come.

Jeff, Logan, Chelsea, and I headed to England to edit another BBC documentary. During my time of sadness, a big fluffy white cat regularly visited us in our little garden suite. It was affectionate and calm, and I would bribe it to stay by doling out kitty treats. It would lie on the bed and purr, bringing a cheerful mood into the room. I felt it was a little angel coming to me with love and allowing me to love it back.

One day, while on a late afternoon walk, Chelsea and I saw a poster advertising a medium who was coming to a church to do a group reading. We talked to Jeff about it and decided it might be an uplifting experience to go, and it was something we wouldn't get the chance to do where we live in Canada.

When the evening arrived, the three of us quietly slipped into the audience. We chose seats somewhere in the middle, wanting to just blend in. It had been a push to get me out into a group of people, as my heart felt like being alone. But we settled in, feeling the anticipation of those around us. With this many people in the room, the odds of getting a message from someone we knew were not high. The medium would likely hear from only a few spirits and would spend time giving their loved ones a warm, unrushed visit with them. It is always enjoyable watching others make a connection.

The medium was just getting into her stride, and there was a really nice flow with Spirit coming through. Then, as if I had drifted into another reality, I heard her say, "I'm hearing, 'Susan, Susan, Susan.' It's a gentleman and it appears that he is hiding in some bushes. Does this make sense to anyone?"

I stared, transfixed. How could it be? Chelsea was poking me, telling me to put my hand up and claim the message. Mediums need to keep the energy flowing and want people to come forth straight away if what they are saying makes sense to them. But I was trying to adjust—it just seemed so fantastic.

As I put my hand up, the medium came to me quickly. She told me that he was an Italian man, dressed very smartly, with beautiful hair. Before I knew him, before his head had been shaved for his first operation, Giorgio had had lovely long black hair that he kept in a ponytail. She saw him come over and kneel down in front of me, and she said, "He has a very intense love for you." I knew that, from his current perspective, he now understood completely the level of spiritual love on which we had connected during our healing experiences. What she must have thought was romantic love I knew to be something very different.

At the end of the evening, I thanked her for sharing her amazing abilities. Jeff then asked her if he could book a private reading for me. She set up a date for the following week.

Relieved and grateful to have the opportunity to possibly talk to Giorgio again, I felt a huge weight begin to lift from my shoulders. Over the next few days I sat quietly by myself, writing out questions I wanted Giorgio to answer. I had been filled with so many doubts since his passing that I felt I had to know a few things before I could move on with my life. I didn't even know if Giorgio would come through in the private reading, but this possibility seemed like my saving grace, and it was all I thought about.

When I got to the reading, the medium, Bernie, didn't seem to recall much about me. I know that when mediums do readings, they are so tuned in to relaying Spirit's message that it just flows through them and then is gone from their consciousness, like water through a funnel. I did not show her my questions or tell her anything about my hopes for the reading. All she asked me was my first name.

Giorgio did come through—he came through for the whole hour. He answered all my questions, one by one, as if he were holding my list in his hand, and then told me so much more. Here is some of what Giorgio had to say, given to me by Bernie and directly transcribed from a recording of the reading:

> There's a man drawing close.
> All of a sudden he has come in like a bolt of lightning.
> He's putting his arms around you and giving you loads of kisses and loads of cuddles.
> This has got to be like a fatherly or brotherly type of figure.

When he's around you, he brings this to you.

I have to sing to you, "You light up my life."

He makes me feel that you lit up his life.

He's taking me to his head.

He's almost making me feel that when he passed, a little bit of you died.

And he wants you to know that he is going to be helping you with your energy.

You were giving him healing while he was here.

He's going to be giving you healing and he's going to be working with your healing.

He's getting trained up, he's telling me.

He likes to repay—it's the love he wants to repay.

He can't thank you enough for the healing.

And written right across my eyes is "It worked." The healing worked.

His transition was so easy.

He didn't actually have to have healing when he went to the other side.

You did it all, this end, for him.

He's very emotional as he draws close here.

He is singing the song "You're beautiful, that's what you are."

Did you say you didn't want any money for doing it?

It's how he's making me feel, like there's no payment there.

"Don't give up on... don't give up."

I don't know if you had some doubts on certain things. Don't give up, all right?

You have a beautiful pathway there.

Have you thought of writing a book?

He says about a book here.

I don't know if it's got twelve chapters.

He's making me feel that his name is going to be in there somewhere.

Have you dedicated something to him?

He knows, because he's talking about you dedicating something to him and he's happy about that too.

You have eight people that work with you, with your healing.

No, sorry, nine... Giorgio just said, "And me."

Nine work with you and your healing, and that team is going to grow.

Life unfolds in ways you couldn't imagine. I had thought it was over when Giorgio died, the end. My path didn't make sense to me anymore; things hadn't worked out the way I thought they were supposed to. Did the universe have a plan? Did my soul have a plan that I had forgotten about? Did Giorgio's and my choices take us on a route I hadn't thought of? But with any route, you are always taken somewhere. I had never conceived of our working partnership in this form, with Giorgio helping from spirit. What I thought was the end was really a whole new beginning.

It's been terribly hard for me to learn to trust and let myself be guided gently along the invisible path of my existence, where my sense of direction comes from my emotional compass held deep within my soul. Fear and grief made me want to stop following my inner voice, but love got me going again. Giorgio found a way to let me know we had a lot of work to do and this was no time for second thoughts.

True to his word, Giorgio helps me all the time. He gives me support in healings and he gives me support in my life. He often comes around on his own, and I call on him when I need him. Although he's not here in a physical body, I still think of Giorgio as one of my best friends.

THE CENTRE

AS MY EXPERIENCE with Giorgio showed, it was hard for me to do healings in our house. It was difficult, amidst all the busyness, to let myself relax into a healing. It was also not good for my family to have to be very conscious of their noise and activity.

Jeff decided to give me an incredible gift: a healing and writing centre. I call it the Centre, but the sign above the door reads *Hazel House*. In England many years before, I had seen the building in a meditation. It is my sacred retreat and I share it with those who need the high frequency of energy it brings forth for their healings. I was once told in a reading that the energy of the Earth around and beneath the Centre could alone heal a person.

From our house, I walk to the Centre on a cedar boardwalk that winds through a thick forest of aspen and red-osier dogwood. The boardwalk circles around a small waterfall and pond and comes to the side of the porch of my beautiful hideaway. Three ten-foot-wide stairs reach down from the front of the porch to the surface of the pond. I can sit on the stairs, just above the water, and transform into a blissful state as I listen to the little waterfall that cascades down to the other side of the pond and watch the colourful koi swim around.

Each wall of the octagonal Centre is eight feet long. The ceiling funnels up to a round skylight. The walls, ceiling, and carpet are a soft white. Simple and uncluttered, the interior allows the purest of energies to flow unencumbered. My healing table lies directly under the skylight in the middle of the room, where natural light streams down. It is an uplifting and peaceful place. The energy inspires me and fills me up for bringing through healing.

Jeff decided to build the Centre just before I was going to start a long and challenging healing with a man who was coming up from the States. At the time, all of our money was tied up in getting our next film going and buying the camera gear we needed for a new project. Thinking it was too much, I tried to talk Jeff out of going ahead. The land had to be cleared of thick bush and trees, many of them fallen and criss-crossed over each other. The pond had to be dug and lined to hold water. Building materials had to be bought, and the Centre, which was quite a difficult plan, had to be built. During the planning stages, I couldn't sleep at all. I would lie awake trying to figure out the finances and the logistics. Every night, I tried to talk Jeff out of it, but he felt very strongly that it would be a big boost to the healings and to me.

I thank Jeff for his courage to move forward and complete the Centre, despite it not being at all feasible on paper. Jeff could clearly see the end result and he wouldn't be slowed down by practicalities. I love him so much for this.

The Centre is the greatest material gift I have ever been given, and has been home to amazing healings. From the basement to the bathroom to my little bit of heaven, my healing spaces have evolved right along with me.

When people come to me for healing, they are often surprised and sometimes uncomfortable that I don't accept money. For me, money does not resonate as part of the equation at any level. I never actually spent time making this decision—it is just what feels completely natural for me. The energy that I experience in the healings is a gift. What I have been able to learn and the insights I have gained into the magnitude of our existence cannot be measured.

Beyond that, I did not study healing in the traditional sense; it is an honour I've been given, and I hope I am doing it justice. I understand that most people who study healing techniques need to make a living from their practice, as they should.

I also know that gratitude is one of the highest-frequency emotions we can practise. To resonate with the healing energy, it is helpful to attune to higher levels of being. I would like people to feel a connection with the healing on an emotional level.

The healing energy itself is worthy of gratitude. When healings are over, I suggest to people that they say, with their hearts and their minds, "I give love and gratitude." It can be to the universe, the Spirit energy, or whatever is meaningful to them. I always send out love and gratitude when I finish a healing. Even though I send it out silently from within, it is a sincere and powerful acknowledgement.

I think that often for people, money replaces gratitude. Many times, when people pay for something, they feel the transaction is complete. I believe that in many areas of our lives, money has taken our awareness away from the importance of feeling thankful, thereby eliminating one of the highest-energy opportunities we have available to us.

When money does not enter into it, an energy exchange is created that raises the whole healing experience to another level. The love that people usually reciprocate when they have had this unconditional love given to them freely, as Spirit and Source do, is one of the most wonderful things I have ever been a part of. As Giorgio once expressed it so beautifully to me after a healing: "The love I feel all around me is so incredible, it makes me want to get down on my knees and kiss the ground."

I am fortunate, because of our income as filmmakers, to be able to take part in this interaction of energy without thinking about money or that part of our material lives. This blessing has allowed me to indulge in the love we share, for no other reason than that we can.

MY OWN HEALING

PEOPLE NEED TO heal emotionally in order to heal physically, and in order to heal emotionally they need to connect to their soul's journey. We come to each lifetime for a reason that we ourselves created before we were born—a plan for our physical life that helps guide us on this journey. This journey happens over many lifetimes, but ultimately our purpose here on Earth is to learn to live as close to "being love" as we can. I believe we are meant to feel good, to feel joyful. When we are honest with ourselves, slow down, and allow our inner voice to speak to us, our emotional state can be a gauge of where we are along this path. Our bodies are our vehicles for this trip and they reflect the direction of our journey.

So even though I was a very loving person and the first half of my life had been wonderful, I started having issues with my health. Before I met Hazel, I was living according to my plan: setting up my life, having a family, and being there for Jeff, Chelsea, and Logan. By starting my exploration of energy on physical, emotional, and spiritual levels, I had made a fundamental shift in my life, yet I was not allowing myself to move forward at an even pace. I kept pulling my energy back when I felt uncertainty or fear. When I did so, I felt unhappy because I was not trusting my soul's voice, and my energy frequency would slow down. This low frequency started to block the flow of energy in my body, and I developed various health issues.

Ultimately, health issues became one of my greatest teachers.

What I have found with people who come for healing is that each has their own level of commitment to healing. The initial healing of the physical is the easiest, because with the help of the energy from Source and Spirit, the frequency of the energy in the body's cells can be increased fairly rapidly. Next, the blocked emotional energy from the past has to be removed. But for ultimate physical health, I believe we have to be on track with our higher purpose.

What I have found to be true for myself is that the degree of my commitment to healing is equal to the degree of my honesty with myself about what I truly feel. As I experienced these health issues, what I felt, deep down, was fear of telling my story to the world and writing my book. I was battling a fear that was controlling my ability to move forward in my life. It was so much easier to keep my story a secret, but I had to be willing to just be and listen to my soul's voice. I had to be willing to change the aspects of my life that were not in alignment with the life I had intended. This, for me, meant coming out of the closet and sharing my truth with the world: all that I had come to understand about the nature of our existence. I knew that if I had the courage to let everything go and allow the truth to come through, I would heal.

I called everyone to the kitchen table for lunch. Our latest film project had been stressful for Jeff and me, and I was trying to remain positive and optimistic. As I sat down, pausing for a moment as everyone else got settled for their meal, I rested my hand across my neck. Under my thumb, I felt a lump the size of a walnut at the base of my throat. I could not believe it—I had to be wrong. But even as I thought this, I knew I was absolutely correct.

At that moment, everything in my life took on a different perspective. I knew this lump could not be good. I knew that I was now facing a whole new set of challenges and that if only I could turn back the clock, I would welcome having just my old stresses. My reality had shifted and I sat transfixed, finding it hard to believe this lump could really be there. Then, without hesitation, I announced my discovery to everyone at the table. Maybe they would tell me that I was wrong and the lump was normal, that everyone had one and I didn't know it. But they confirmed what I already knew: it wasn't normal.

A film editor was staying with us for a few weeks as we finished a film about searching for a grizzly bear in the mountains near our home. It was inspired by a story by Aldo Leopold about the last grizzly bear in Arizona in the early 1900s. Jeff had always been moved by Aldo's story, not only because of his great love and admiration for the bears, but also because the story is a poignant look at the loss of the heart and soul of the mountains when the wildlife is gone. This is especially true for an animal as powerful as the grizzly, whose energy is amplified across the land, proclaiming a greatness on the Earth far beyond our human influence.

After lunch, I made an appointment to see a doctor right away. I couldn't stop touching the lump and I was surprised that I hadn't noticed it before. I needed to know what it was and if it could be easily treated. I just wanted it out of my life.

The doctor was a lovely young woman with so much responsibility and so many patients that I was lucky to get five minutes of her time. I received each piece of her information in rapid succession: yes, you have a lump growing at the base of your throat; it could be a nodule on your thyroid; it's probably not cancer, but you will need further testing to determine if it's malignant; the first step is to book you for an ultrasound.

The ultrasound showed a large, rapidly growing nodule. The doctor suggested two tests to determine if it was cancerous: a biopsy and a radioactive screening, in two different cities at different hospitals. They would call me to set up the appointments. In the meantime, the doctor said, if the nodule grew so quickly that I was having trouble swallowing or talking, they could operate, removing it with a good portion of my thyroid.

As I got into the car, my first response was to cry. I couldn't get my mind around what she had told me. Alone for the thirty-minute drive home, I had time to think. Between spells of tears, all I arrived at was the notion that I had been given time to heal this situation on my own.

Chelsea researched the top thyroid doctors and found a highly recommended naturopathic doctor in Vancouver. I managed to get an appointment within a few weeks and went with Jeff down to the coast. The doctor did blood tests and said that he was sure he could help me with a plant-based thyroid supplement. He also explained the difficulty with the two further tests the doctor had suggested: they were inconclusive and could give only a percentage reflecting the likelihood that the growth was cancerous. Radioactive screening was also unhealthy for my thyroid and would be hard on it. As my thyroid was already struggling, I did not want to make it harder for it to recover. Plus, it would make it more difficult for me to stay focused on healing if I were told there was a 30 percent likelihood of cancer based on the screening results.

I decided to start with three modes of healing: taking the supplements from the naturopath, changing my diet to be more alkaline, and bringing healing energy into myself in meditation and from the Earth. With the meditation, I opened up my crown chakra, linked into the healing energy of my higher self, and connected with Spirit and Source energy to raise my energy to a place of healing. The Earth healing I did by lying on the ground every day in a beautiful grassy place by my pond. I visualized the healing energy of the Earth in all its pureness and power, deep energy coming up through the beautiful Earth quickening my energy and restoring it to a place of wellness. This was carried out more by sensing the energy than by intellectualizing it. I felt that the energy that was available, both from Source and from the Earth, was there for me if I could be in the right emotional place to connect with its frequency. I had to shift my energy so that it resonated with these energies. I needed to be one with them, not separate. Just as I breathe air in and out of my lungs, allowing it to become part of my makeup, I needed to let the flow of energy from the Earth and from Source be an extension of myself. I found that if I could feel this experience and not overthink it, it would have a very restoring effect on me. It takes calmness, acceptance, and an ability to just be.

I wasn't sure of the results, as the growth was still very evident. The hospital kept calling, urging me to come for their tests. I kindly declined, feeling their real concern that I was making the wrong choice. But for me it was correct. I wanted time to understand and let my body heal with the help it needed.

After a few weeks, I decided to go to Victoria to visit Chelsea. She was now eighteen and going to university there, and I loved to visit her as often as I could. It was about a seven-hour journey. On the way, I could feel the lump starting to get in the way of my swallowing. On a basic survival level, it is distressing to feel that your throat is blocked. I kept coughing, trying to clear my throat. I had to pull over and walk around the car in an attempt to clear my mind of worry. I told myself that it wasn't an emergency situation; the lump couldn't grow that fast. But alone on a long drive, with miles to think, I had to remind myself emphatically that this lump would dissolve when I had aligned myself with the complete combination needed for my well-being. It is important to say that this was my choice for my specific medical condition, not my recommendation for other people. Everyone needs to do what feels right for their own healing.

In Victoria, Chelsea was at school during the day, so I had time to myself. I pondered the missing piece of the puzzle: why had this nodule grown in my throat in the first place? I understood that my thyroid was out of balance. But why? What was the underlying reason I was out of balance? There can be more than one thing contributing to a problem, and I did not want to miss any of them.

I found a book on chakras. The growth was in my throat chakra. One cause of blocked energy in the throat chakra is suppressed communication. The energy around your throat is related to your voice. If you are not listening to your own voice, the energy that flows through this vortex can become blocked. There are a range of emotions a person could be experiencing that prevent them from freely speaking their truth or even listening to it themselves. These emotions could be self-doubt, insecurity, powerlessness, fear, or other self-limiting feelings. These emotions have a slower frequency of energy that will create slower energy in the cells and therefore ill health.

I had been so busy helping my family, doing healings, and working on our latest film that I had completely stopped writing. I held all of my inspiration inside, denying it the chance to come out. I did feel desperate to write, but everything else took priority. I also lacked the fundamental conviction that it mattered whether I wrote or not. Not writing was the biggest mistake I was continually making. I felt such a strong desire to write, it literally pulsed through my veins. That was all the justification I should have needed, that it was something I needed to do for myself. But because I had no guarantee that my writing would be useful to anyone else, it was hard to commit valuable time to it. This had to change. Yes, I had a lot of demands on my time, but if writing would help heal me, surely I should rethink my priorities and find the time to write.

I also decided to take advantage of being in a city and seek out a healing massage therapist. Chelsea knew of a woman named Linda who had a good reputation, so I made an appointment with her for treatments on my neck and back.

I felt it was important to get energy movement in these areas through a combination of methods.

I was very pleased that she was able to fit me in for an appointment. She settled me on her healing table. I explained the growth on my thyroid and that I needed work on my neck and back. A sympathetic person, she cared deeply about my situation. As she was working on my neck, I lay with my eyes closed. I soon became aware of the presence of an Asian woman sitting to my right towards the end of the healing table. She was in Spirit energy. She had long black hair and her head was bent slightly. I couldn't seem to interact with her in my mind; she appeared very still, in quiet thought. Then I noticed that she was holding a small boy, about ten months old, in her left arm. He was lively and smiling at me. Although I saw the woman and the boy as energetic beings in my mind's eye, they were very clear, as if they were physically there. I didn't know who they were, and wondered if they might be people from the neighbourhood who had passed and were still hanging around in spirit form.

I wondered if I should mention them to Linda. I had no idea what she thought of Spirit energy; many people have a hard time understanding and relating to the spirit world. But, I told myself, if having blocked throat chakra energy was about not communicating and expressing what was important to me, then this was a really good time to start sharing.

After the healing, I told Linda about the woman and child I had seen. She was grateful for the information as she couldn't see spirits herself. Linda was sure the woman was the spiritual goddess Kuan Yin and that I had seen her energetic frequency, the energy that her representation manifested. My description of the woman fit Kuan Yin.

Linda had studied many healing techniques in Asia and felt a strong connection to and respect for Kuan Yin, who has her foundations in the East. She had asked Kuan Yin to come and extend energy for the healing on me.

She asked me if I knew of Kuan Yin and I said that I did not. Linda took me to her reception area and showed me a statue of Kuan Yin. Although it did look different from the woman I had seen in spirit, as it was an interpretive statue, both were Asian women with long black hair. The woman of the statue wore her hair up and did not have a baby, but Linda was certain I had seen Kuan Yin. The name did not register with me, and although I was grateful for the healing and the experience of seeing her, I soon let thoughts of her go.

After a couple of days I returned for another session with Linda. During the two hours, we discovered many tight muscles that were painful to release. When we finished, I felt I needed to go for a little walk to clear my mind before driving home. I wandered into a little shop. I had no particular interest in going there, it was just on my path. There, on the top shelf, facing the door, was a statue of an Asian lady holding a baby in her left arm. When I looked up into her beautiful porcelain face, I heard her say, "It's me, it's me. You did see me. I'm the one with the baby." Recognizing her as Kuan Yin, I felt completely overcome. There was an energy around her that pulsed into me, giving me the message that this was important and I should pay attention.

The shop owner could see how moved I was by the statue and offered to sell it to me for half price. I was so dazed that I just smiled, thanked him, and left the store.

When I got back to Chelsea's apartment, I made lunch and tried to quiet myself down. Thoughts of this meeting with Kuan Yin danced around in my head and I couldn't relax. I decided to phone Jeff, as I couldn't wait to share this exciting experience.

I told Jeff the whole story of Kuan Yin, starting with seeing her at Linda's. When I was finished, Jeff thought for a couple of seconds and then asked me if I remembered the first psychic reading I'd had many years before. That medium had told me that I would be doing some writing and that a guide named Kuan Yin would work with me. Now that Jeff mentioned it, I remembered that message. At the time, it had been lost on me because I wasn't writing and had never heard of Kuan Yin. But now I saw it in a much different light. I had been writing off and on for a while, and I felt that much of my writing was inspirational writing, but I didn't know where it was coming from. Now I feel that much of my writing is inspired by the energetic frequency that Kuan Yin expresses.

By now my excitement was building. Jeff could not believe that I hadn't purchased the statue—and neither could I. I headed right back downtown. Parking in Victoria can be hard to find, but when I got to the parking lot, I not only found a parking space, I also found a free ticket in the machine, left by a kind person because it hadn't expired. Everything was lining up for me. I got to the shop, fearful that the statue might have been sold, but there she was, waiting for me to receive her message and move forward.

I still knew little about Kuan Yin and was anxious to learn anything I could. After putting the statue in the car, I went across the street to a little spiritual shop to look for some information. The woman who worked there said she didn't have any books on Kuan Yin but wrote her name down and suggested I look on the Internet. As I was leaving, she said,

"Don't you know who Kuan Yin is? She's the goddess of love and compassion."

I almost couldn't hide my excitement and sheer amazement, because I remembered having lunch with Jeff at the art gallery and seeing the title of my book: *Conscious Evolution*. Since then, I had come to understand, through my writing, that the human species is meant to be consciously evolving from a place of fear to one of love and compassion.

I wanted to dance down the street and hug everyone I saw. I wanted to stand on the rooftops and call out, "Do you know how wonderful life is?" I felt intensely that anything is possible if we just pay attention and let ourselves go with it. This other realm, this other dimension, this energy—it's there for us, wanting to help us and guide us on our way. We just have to allow it. We have to be aware and let go of this struggle we hold on to. My joy couldn't be described in words. It was as if life were limitless. I had glimpsed a whole other perspective. I wanted to get on this energy wavelength and never get off.

The energy of Kuan Yin resonates with the frequency of Universal Love, and connecting with it created the same profound experience. The energy surrounding and coming from Kuan Yin was so powerful that when I connected to it and recognized it, it was a catalyst projecting me in the direction of my unknown path.

I had gone for treatment to unlock my muscles and get the energy flowing through my body more easily. I had thought that if my throat chakra was blocked, the massage treatment would help the energy around my neck start to move more fluidly and my thyroid would heal. And I am sure it was very beneficial in this way. But even more importantly, going to see Linda reconnected me to Kuan Yin and made me believe that my writing might have purpose. Maybe I could justify taking time to write. Maybe it wasn't true that everything else was a bigger priority or that it was selfish to take this time for myself. This growth in my throat had led me to seek answers for my healing, and this, in turn, guided me along my life path.

To heal is to feel intense love and compassion, and there is no greater love than that of a higher-vibrational being and the energy of Source itself. In my understanding, this high-vibrational healing energy enables people to experience love in the purest form: a love obtainable by all, a love at the core of every being. We can all open ourselves to its radiance and let it flow to us, if it is our will. Such a life force is available to us without judgment. If we are able to recognize it, remember it, or just allow ourselves to let this love flow through us, I do not believe we would ever go back.

Kuan Yin is a messenger of this love. Even through darkness, she reminds us that there is light if we just open our eyes to it. She is a luminous being radiating loving, compassionate, and healing energy, like the moon reflecting light upon us. She raises our vibration beyond the physical and waits for our awareness to grow so that we may move on to embrace what is possible. What an honour it is to feel the energy of such a being. If she is able to impart her knowing through me—that is, if I am able to allow it to come through in good faith—how blessed I will be for her guidance.

Weeks later, I went for another ultrasound on my neck. I was full of trepidation, although I could no longer feel the nodule in my throat. The ultrasound confirmed that the nodule had entirely disappeared. I had chosen a few different healing options, all of which I believed to be important for a complete healing. I did what felt right for me and what I felt, on an intuitive level, my body would respond to.

As I write at my desk, I look up to see the white porcelain statue of Kuan Yin and the little boy, sitting with grace and looking into the room. I am forever grateful.

TRANSITIONING TO THE AFTERLIFE

CONTINUED TO WRITE more and create more balance in my life, and I still clearly remembered the incredible energy of love that I had experienced with Kuan Yin. But the range of emotional energy that we encounter in our lives kept reminding me what a challenge life is and how much I have to learn. The trick is to keep our balance in a sea of emotions that come in unexpected waves and to learn to navigate through them.

Years after that trip to Victoria, two unusual experiences took me on emotional journeys on a very different spectrum from the enlightened one I had with Kuan Yin. At the same time, they were incredibly special in their own way, helping me to deepen my appreciation of the challenges other people face.

Two men, both strangers to me, who had nothing to do with each other and whose lives I became involved with only after they were physically dead, paid me visits at different times.

Does that sound complicated, crazy, or like a premise for a mystery novel? Maybe all of the above, but for me it was a great lesson in understanding our spirit energy in difficult circumstances and how healing continues even after we've left the physical body. On a personal level, it also helped me gain confidence in my ability to connect to Spirit. It had been many years since my time at the Arthur Findlay College and I was continuing to develop my skills of linking with the spiritual realm. However, I was about to have experiences I didn't think I was capable of.

First, one summer's evening a young man crashed over the abutment of a bridge with his all-terrain vehicle and plunged to his death. He was found face down in the creek below, dead from the impact or from drowning. This accident took place about five kilometres from our home. I couldn't shake the unsettling sensation that his spirit was stuck at the scene. But I didn't have any experience with this, so I tried to ignore my thoughts about him. Then Leanne called and told me that she kept getting the feeling I should go up to the creek.

So Jeff and I went up together. He stayed on the bridge while I hiked down the bank to sit just above the water. It was tricky making my way down the steep slope and over the big rocks, but I felt that I should be close to the bottom of the ravine. I didn't have any experience with something like this, but as in everything I do, I went with how I felt and what seemed natural. I sensed there was a person here feeling alone and confused. I couldn't see an image of his physical body, but if he was there in spirit, I could talk to him. So, because this was all new to me, I followed my instincts on how to connect with him.

I sat quietly and asked if he was there and if he would like to join me. I soon felt the presence of his spirit next to me. I asked him if he knew he was dead. I thought that maybe he remained here in spirit because he still saw himself in physical form and didn't realize he had left his body.

I didn't know what it was like being him, so I thought this was a good opening line. But when I said, "Do you know you are dead?" he replied with an abrupt, "Duh." I was surprised and later amused. Given the gravity of the situation, I thought our conversation would start a little more seriously or philosophically.

He said he was lonely. He told me a few trivial things about himself, such as the fact that he liked pizza. I then said that he didn't need to remain here and that we should look for a light he could go towards. It would take him to a place for those on the spirit level. This is something I had heard of other mediums doing. I looked out and in my mind's eye saw an elderly man standing at the top of a staircase. He seemed to be this young man's grandfather. He was reaching down, his hand extended. His grandson climbed up, grasped his hand, and was gone.

I was surprised that it all happened so quickly and easily. I thought it would have been a big deal, requiring a major effort, but it was straight to the point. I sat there for a while, wanting to make certain I'd got it right. I could no longer feel the presence of his spirit; it felt that he had truly left. I think it was probably easy because he hadn't left his body long before and because he wanted to go. Also, because the accident was unexpected and he died so quickly, perhaps he was confused and his spirit wasn't sure where he was. He just needed some help connecting the two energy levels, the physical and the spiritual.

It was such an interesting and magical event, and it left me wondering if I'd really witnessed it. Wanting some confirmation of what I had experienced, I found his obituary in the newspaper. All it said was that he was survived by his father, mother, siblings, and grandmother. I took from this that his grandfather had already passed away.

The next man was found by a friend of mine. He had hanged himself in a park, and she was the first to happen upon him as she was out walking her dogs. She later called me to say that every time she did yoga, he would appear to her. Her quiet state of mind during yoga made it easy for him to come through. She wanted him to move on. I told her I would do what I could to help her.

Because I felt really protective towards her and my experience was limited, I jumped right into a meditation without asking my guides to surround me with higher energy of love and light to protect me in case he had died in a state of lower emotional energy. I went straight to him in my mind and spirit and made a connection. I asked him to stay away from my friend and said I would help him travel beyond the physical. I did visualizations of helping him go to the higher frequency of the spirit realm, and I thought all was complete.

Soon after, Jeff and I travelled first to Vancouver and then on to Vancouver Island. It was on Vancouver Island that this man had hanged himself.

While Jeff did some business in Vancouver, I waited for him in the car. I started having feelings of complete despair, terrible sensations of powerlessness, a conviction that no matter what I did, people would still automatically judge me and would never give me a chance to prove myself. I felt as though I could never reach better circumstances in my life because other people would always keep me in this lower place. I knew these weren't my feelings or experiences—this man's emotions seemed to be overtaking me. His emotional energy field was infusing mine, and I experienced his sense of desperation as if it were my own. When Jeff got back to the car, I was in tears. Seeing the seriousness of the situation, Jeff took me to a park so I could get into nature. Nature always helps to bring me around when I'm down. He urged me to walk around with him, but I couldn't shake this sense of impending doom.

We decided to catch a ferry to Victoria right away. As we drove onto the ferry, I became fearful. I told Jeff that there was no way I could go up on deck, and asked him to stay close to me. I felt an intense desire to jump overboard. It would be so fast and then everything would be over.

Realizing that this situation was getting out of control, I closed my eyes and begged for help from my guides. I pleaded with them to come and collect this man and take him away, take him to the other side, take him anywhere, but please free me from the burden of his darkness.

While my eyes were closed, I saw three bright flashes of light. Then I felt a change come over me. I opened my eyes and asked Jeff if the ferry attendant had flashed a light into our vehicle. He said no. My spirit guides or someone from Spirit had taken the man away from me and, I believe, helped him find his way to the other side so he would no longer be attached to the physical world. I think he had attached himself to me because I had come to him as a light of love. I think it was as if he was lost and saw a light and went to it for help. Perhaps after he died he was unable to find his way. I believe that when you pass in a lower emotional state, it may take a while to realign yourself and find your way from the physical world to the spiritual. He most likely saw my friend as a bright light to follow, and then, when I reached out to him, he came to me. Because I purposely tried to connect to him and didn't think of setting any boundaries, he linked into my energy field.

I learned a few important lessons from this experience. The first is that we simply can't imagine how other people feel or understand the hold their emotional state has on them unless we've walked in their spirit. Second, we need to be extremely careful about the energy we let ourselves encounter. Since this experience, I always ask for the protection of my guides before I enter other people's energy fields. I've experienced very dark energy coming off people during healings, and it had a dramatic effect on me. I need to remember that although light and love are the most powerful energy, dark energy can be quite strong as well. Lastly, I know my guides were with me during this encounter, but they wanted me to experience the lower energies of emotion to further my understanding of the spectrum of emotions that people live with. The time I spent with this man gave me a great deal of sympathy for him and his state of mind at the time of his death.

A few years later, I hosted Bernie, the English medium who had brought through Giorgio, to come and do readings for people at my house. She had read at least twelve people in about seven days when she came to talk something over with me. She said that two men, in spirit, had been staying quite close to her since she had started the readings the week before. She couldn't figure out who they were with, and every time she did a reading, she expected them to come forward, but they didn't. She went on to say that one man had drowned and the other had hanged himself. The first man was shown to her face down in water. I thought for a minute and said that it was possible they were here for me.

I had a reading the next day and they both came forward and identified themselves by showing her how they had died. This was the only way I would recognize them, because I knew so little about them; it was their deaths that had brought us together. They both thanked me for what I had done for them. I was so grateful for what they had shared with me about their situation in death because it helped me grow as a person and as a healer.

I couldn't believe all the effort they had gone through to let me know they were there. They persevered for days in order to get their message of appreciation to me, and then they were both gone. I am so glad they didn't give up, because it made a big difference to me to know I had really connected to them.

LIFE AFTER LIFE

THE *Oxford English Dictionary* defines "reincarnation" as "the rebirth of a soul in a new body." Although most people can grasp this basic idea, understanding *why* our soul would be reborn in a new body and what happens between lifetimes gives us insight into how we should approach our life.

It took me some time to warm up to the idea that we might live multiple lives, mostly because I really didn't fancy the thought of coming back and doing it all again. And I clearly remember wondering why people cared if there was such a thing as reincarnation. I couldn't understand how knowing if it was true had any value for my life. Now I realize that it has a profound impact, both on the life I'm living and on my perspective.

In the big picture of my soul, my physical body and my material existence in this life are no more than one chapter in a book; whereas my emotional and spiritual body, which creates my energetic experience, is hugely important as I move through one lifetime to another, or from one chapter to the next in a very long book. I feel that we come back to live new experiences in a different physical body so that we can have the opportunity to become more evolved emotionally.

I visualize each chapter taking us farther along on our journey. I believe we write the plan for our next life, or the next chapter, before we are born into it. This includes deciding on the timeline and the possible opportunities or challenges that we will meet along the way.

In our physical life, once we have started on the next section of our journey, and regardless of what we intended in our plan before birth, we always have free will to make choices, and so does everyone whom we engage with along the way. Once we are born into our physical body, it is very difficult not to see ourselves foremost as a physical being with a much different set of priorities. We may be trying to break negative patterns from previous lives, but our ability to feel and listen to what we really know to be true, and not let ourselves be totally consumed by our ego, is very difficult. There is so much fear energy in our human existence that it is challenging to always follow our inner sense of what we want to be doing. But if we could see ourselves, remember ourselves, as spirit beings, our perspective would be much different and our decisions about how we live would be clearer.

We create physical lives because they give us continuous opportunity to choose emotional responses. Because we are so aware of time in our physical lives, choice and consequence become quite obvious. This allows us to see on a very determined scale how our emotional state affects us, those around us, and the physical world we live in. Physical change is much easier to measure than emotional change, but emotional energy determines our physical outcome. Physical matter just gives us a tangible measuring stick, as does time.

At age twenty, we see a person as an adult and just

beginning to learn. By the age of fifty, we would expect that person to be gaining insight into life and what it means; and we think of our elders as being even wiser. A lifetime is a very distinct thing, and most people have the sense that they are meant to be learning something on a deeper level—on an emotional or spiritual plane, rather than just physical skills. We value this aspect of our life, often without really understanding why, but our higher self knows that this is our goal in life: to evolve and to learn.

When Hazel came through with a message for us just a few days after she had died, what she said was very enlightening. The first thing Hazel told us was that her life review had gone well. She had moved into the spiritual realm and was now examining how she had chosen to live her life. A life review allows us to understand the consequences of all our actions. It is also a new starting place of understanding, where we can seek to improve ourselves as emotional and spiritual beings. In much the same way that looking over a marked exam can show us how we could have improved our answers, in a life review we are marking ourselves. As we go through our review, checking our responses to the life situation we were presented with, we feel how we made others feel. Be it positive or negative, we witness our impact on the world.

The frequency of the emotions we practise in our life— our vibration—determines the energetic level we will enter in the spiritual realm. It's my understanding that in the spiritual realm there are many levels. Each is a level of being created by increasing energetic frequency. The level of emotional frequency we are emitting is what mainly affects our soul's journey. Therefore, our journey into the spiritual realm will be at the energy level we are emanating. Like our physical life, our spiritual existence and experience resonates with our own frequency of energy. When we are reborn or reincarnated, we start our new physical life at whatever level of energy we have attained so far from our previous physical lives and in spiritual form. When people talk about karma in our next life, to me they are talking about the frequency of the energy we have created around ourselves. We create our karma by the energy we choose to live by.

So even if at our core we come from Universal or Source energy, our life surrounds us in an energy whose frequency is determined by the choices we have made. As this energy affected our physical life, so will it affect our spiritual life. Because Hazel lived in a place of love, she resonated and therefore experienced a higher level of light and love in spirit. It's not that God loves anyone any less or more—it's simply that we go to the level of frequency that we resonate with.

We may decide to put very big challenges in our own path so as to push ourselves to reach our highest level. So, when very difficult things happen to really wonderful people, it does not necessarily mean they have brought some sort of bad karma on themselves. It could mean that they are challenging themselves. Just as mountain climbers pick more and more difficult ascents because they want to push themselves to be the very best they can be, so we create lives with increasingly difficult routes.

The comforts of our material world by no means reflect the frequency of our spirit. The old soul comes to the physical stage in various costumes—many of which, I'm sure, are not very glamorous. I think high-frequency souls sometimes choose to share their lifetime with people who still exist in lower frequencies in order to help them raise themselves to higher levels. This will, I feel, often put them in harm's way in their physical life as they try to bring light into darkness. We all have recognized beautiful souls living in very difficult situations. It's not that they are suffering karma for something they did in a previous life; instead, it is possible they are raising the frequency of energy to help those who are ready for change. It is their emotional and spiritual awareness, not their physical life circumstances, that helps us understand the level they have attained.

I realize and appreciate that what I have written here about reincarnation is at the most basic level, and there is a lot more to it. For example, I feel that the energy of our soul or the thread of Universal energy that creates our consciousness could exist in different ways or, in a sense, in different places at the same time. Perhaps one form of our soul's energy lives this physical life while another fragment or form exists in the spiritual energetic realm. This could be the connection between our physical self and our higher self, the part that communicates with us through our emotions, rallying us to live the life we had intended.

I don't think it really matters right now if I don't have all the answers about reincarnation. What I'm meant to understand is only that we are emotional and spiritual beings living lives in order to become self-aware—aware of who we really are and of our evolutionary journey towards consciously living at much higher levels of emotional frequency. Understanding the purpose of living many lives in physical bodies accelerates our emotional development and makes the benefits of being mindful of reincarnation quite obvious.

I fully realize that if I am not able to do my very best and move as far from my fear-based emotions as I can in this life, I'll be trying to move through them again next time around. So I want to be conscious of why I am making the choices I am, and I want to make sure they come from my heart and soul and are not a consequence of fears I may be holding on to, fears that could hold me back from allowing myself to be the best I can be in this life. Otherwise, I'll just be creating a redo for myself.

So I'm all in during this life. And not just for myself, but for the planet and everyone I share it with, as my energy intermingles into the oneness of us all.

MY EARTH MEDITATION

WHEN I WAS a child, maybe ten years old, I thought that our bodies were like miniature Earths. Our blood was the rivers and creeks; our bones were the rocks; our breath was the air and wind. I thought that if we could learn to look after our bodies, we could learn to look after the Earth.

This memory was brought back to me in an unusual way. At our little local grocery store, I met up with a truckful of bear hunters buying fuel before heading out into the forest. Men, women, and their children, all dressed in camouflage, held their guns between their knees, intent on killing a bear on a beautiful sunny afternoon. They were from out of town, on a holiday. It was an absolutely soul-destroying sight. How could they want to kill something just for fun and take their children along to witness it?

I forced myself to ask the driver, who was filling the truck with gas, to think about the beauty of the bear, maybe to take pictures, or at least to respect our neighbourhood. I even offered him a copy of one of our bear films; maybe if the families watched it, they would reconsider their hunt. I hoped that if I looked into his eyes, I would find a thread of goodness. I did not. He smirked and told me they would never change their minds. His soul was cloaked in layers of slow-vibrational energy, maybe accumulated over lifetimes, and no love or gratitude for life was to be found in his energy field. The memory of the bear hunters haunts me still.

I do not think talking to them did any good, and it left me trying to comprehend how we can elevate the human consciousness when such low levels of humanity are abundant. I know that if you send your thoughts, which are energy, out to something, you are sending it energy. If there is something in your life or future you don't want and you keep thinking about it, you are sending it energy. Instead, you must think about and therefore send energy to what you *do* want.

The bear hunters were a symbol of the disrespect so much of humanity seems to have for the Earth and the natural world. And at times, the sense of this attitude is too overwhelming for me and I feel the Earth will not be able to heal from the pain we have inflicted upon it. At these times, I have to remember how I see a person who comes for healing. I don't connect with the disease that seems to be overtaking that person's body, but rather I put my energy into seeing the health that is possible. This incident reminded me of my childhood theory that our bodies are like the Earth. Focusing on well-being comes naturally during a healing; I am drawn to people on a soul level, and in that connection there is only wellness.

Therefore, when I focus on the Earth, I send my highest frequency of energy outwards, surrounding the Earth with love, peace, and joy. And all the people, animals, and elements of the natural world that are in vibrational alignment with such frequencies can come together. As I do a meditation for the Earth, I expand my energy of love: out past the area where I am sitting, out through the valley, up over the mountains, upwards into the sky, until I can visualize the Earth in space. I surround it in beautiful green light for healing or pink light for love. I see the Earth as completely pure and healthy, radiating its beautiful energy out to the universe.

The bear hunters were a graphic reminder that if I direct my energy at such a low level of humanity, I will destroy myself. Then I will be of no help to animals, people, or the Earth, but instead a drag on their energy. The only way forward is to rejoice with gratitude and love for the beauty that surrounds our Earth. With every thought of that beauty, it will expand, for our thoughts create waves of manifestation and our world is created as we see it. Not only is the energy we send to the Earth important for its health, but the high-frequency energy the Earth is sending us is critical for our health. The healthier the Earth, the higher the frequency of energy we can experience from it. I've always wanted to protect the Earth and the wild things, but I have also been aware that the Earth has healing to offer me. If we resonate with the power of the Earth's energy, we can revitalize ourselves back to a state of well-being. The natural world has healed me emotionally throughout my life, giving me the strength to get through very difficult times. I have read of people who have done nothing but lie on the Earth to heal themselves of life-threatening illnesses. The Earth heals the body, mind, and soul.

Most of our human world is artificial. We have become disconnected from our Earth and the animals we share it with. Often, when I hear of people searching for something they feel deep down is missing from their lives, I think that what they're looking for is their relationship to the natural world. At our very core, as physical beings, we are meant to have a profound union with the Earth. Just a few generations ago we lived very much as part of nature, but now many children are raised separate from it. A lot of people have become dissociated from the very thing that keeps them alive.

We can all tap into nature's incredible energy. We're meant to be a part of it. Soak it in, with love and gratitude.

I AM LOVE

CONTINUED TO FEEL nervous as I moved further towards a life of healing and writing and away from film-making. Although I was still helping Jeff with our films, my heart wasn't in it. I had been a film producer all my adult life. I took pride in the films we made, in the fact that I was an accomplished professional and that I worked with Jeff. People saw us a filmmaking team. But filmmaking started to lose its meaning for me. Feeling myself separating from it scared me, because I thought I would be left with nothing. Who would I be?

One day when I was by myself, the fear suddenly overwhelmed me. I went for a long walk. I walked and walked, and I thought, *Oh my God, I don't know who I am anymore. I don't know what I feel a part of now. Who am I? I'm nobody. I'm coming to the middle of my life and what am I?* Overcome with uneasiness, I started crying. I turned back and headed for home. When I got there, I sat in the kitchen, feeling very much alone, asking, *Who am I, who am I?* It was a desperate plea to myself. I was soul-searching in the most profound sense.

And then I heard a voice in my mind gently say, "Who are you?"

I thought, *Well, I'm Sue Turner.*

"That's your name. Who are you?"

Well, I'm a mother for Chelsea and Logan, and I'm Jeff's wife.

"That's who you share your life with. Who are you?"

Well, I'm a film producer.

"That's what you do for a living. Who are you?"

I was getting a little impatient. *Well, I'm a country woman in her fifties.*

"That's your physical description. Who are you?"

I went very still. I went as deep inside myself and as far as I could go, breaking down all the outside barriers, asking myself over and over, *Who am I?* If I could really take away everything else about myself so that all that was left was a single thread of truth, what was the one thing I really knew about myself? The one thing I could say for sure, truthfully, from the heart? The one thing I knew I was?

I thought, *I am love.*

I love deeply and I have so much love to give. I know that love is the very core of my being. I thought with certainty, *I am love.*

And I heard the voice say, "Yes, you are love. That's who you are."

Now, this may all sound quite simple, but it was a life-changing breakthrough for me. When we realize who we are at our essence, then we know what we need to stay true to. In life, that's all that really matters. If we live the love we are, in everything we do, then we are being true to ourselves.

Whatever hat I'm wearing, I know what's underneath: one big love.

THE POWER OF EMOTIONAL ENERGY

Jeremy

JEREMY CAME TO me out of sheer desperation. He didn't know where else to turn. He had cancer throughout his abdomen, and he had been told that, at stage four, it was too far along to operate.

Jeremy was nineteen when I first met him. He had come to live with us for a few weeks out in our island camp when we were filming the white spirit bears. He had such a big, cheery smile and a sparkle in his eyes. I remember well how much he liked to eat my homemade cookies after a long day of filming. He also loved Chelsea, who was only about a year old at the time. He called her "the Chelsmeister," lingo from *Saturday Night Live*. But on the serious side, he wanted to talk with Jeff and me about what he should do in his life. He wanted to make sure he chose something responsible and also meaningful. He was still so young, and yet filled with concern about making the right choices

When Jeremy arrived for healing, he was thin, tired, and in a great deal of pain. He had trouble walking and couldn't eat because his intestine was blocked by a cancer growth.

He was very scared and did not feel up to visiting with my family on the first evening, so I took him to a quiet room to talk. He told me he felt he was outside his body. He bowed his head and cried.

Jeremy listed nine symptoms resulting from the cancer. One, which really worried him, was a cancerous fluid in his abdomen; the doctor had said it would continue to increase as the disease intensified. He already felt bloated from it.

We started the healings the next morning. I was totally focused on the need to heal his physical body. Nothing else seemed to matter at that point; this was an emergency situation. The healings were rapid, taking place directly on the areas of the cancer, and results came quickly. The cancerous fluid began to disappear. This was very exciting, as the fluid seemed to be a symbol of the cancer for both Jeremy and myself. Within three days, Jeremy could run a few kilometres. It was absolutely astounding. Not only was he running, but he was running in snow with his winter boots on. His joy was palpable. He had little pain, he was eating well, he was having bowel movements. You could see the life returning to him. A few days later, the nausea had abated, he was able to sleep well and was no longer having night sweats, and the fluid was entirely gone from his abdomen. At around seven days, eight of Jeremy's symptoms were gone; he had only a slight discomfort in one area of his intestine.

In this first visit, we had concentrated on getting rid of the physical symptoms of the cancer. His physical body seemed to respond quickly to the healing energy, but I wasn't prepared for the bigger picture. Jeremy's case turned out to be much more about emotional healing and how critical this is for physical wellness. Although the healings to release the cancer were very significant, the emotional healing came much more slowly.

Jeremy's most obvious emotion was fear: fear of dying and fear of leaving his family. For both of these, the spirit world came through in the most incredible and unexpected way. We were only a couple of days into the healing when Jeremy felt well enough to take an evening walk. He and Jeff had gone into town that day, as Jeremy was excited about grocery shopping for his new-found appetite. On the way back, Jeremy asked to be let out of the car a couple of kilometres from our home so he could walk. It was a dark winter night and it was snowing. Had I been driving, I don't think I would have let him out to walk home alone, but Jeff was comfortable with Jeremy's decision and saw his excitement over his recovery.

Jeremy later described to me how he felt somewhat anxious as Jeff drove away, wondering if he had the strength to walk all the way to our house. Three days before, he had hardly been able to walk up our front steps. Now here he was, on his own, with two kilometres to go on a winter's night.

As he was thinking about how he felt very much alone, he suddenly became aware of his great-grandfather's presence walking along beside him. Instantly, he was awash in sensations of calmness and security. He felt every detail of his great-grandfather, and as he closed his eyes and walked, it was as if his grandfather was right there, still in his physical body. Jeremy could even smell the smoke from his pipe. He let Jeremy know he was not alone, not only on this winter's night but also on his journey of healing.

When Jeremy came through our kitchen door about forty minutes later, he was full of light and joy. He wanted me to go with him right away to the healing centre. We walked on a trail cut through two feet of fluffy new snow. At the Centre, excitement and happiness pulsed out of Jeremy. He was ecstatic as he relayed his experience to me. It was by far our happiest time; we were connected and felt complete love and support from the spirit world.

We had a long talk, basking in the wonder of how magical and surreal it is when the spiritual energy of the ones we love joins us. It was as if a huge weight had been lifted from Jeremy, as he realized how powerful are the energies of this once-hidden world.

On our walk back to the house, the beauty of nature, the night, and the snow added to our joy and childlike intrigue. We both spontaneously fell on our backs and made snow angels, laughing at how fun and crazy we felt. Spirit energy can give you a wonderful high.

Throughout the healings, Jeremy continued to be visited by family and friends in spirit. Neither of us had expected this, and it was incredibly special. Except for Dana, I had not done healings with anyone who could connect with Spirit the way Jeremy could. Every healing felt like a reunion, and it was so amazing to hear what Jeremy had seen. His grandparents came every time, along with some old friends. Jeremy would describe in great detail everything about them: what they wore, where they sat, what they said, and what they did. The two of us were part of a much larger team. The energy for the healing was abundant and the success we were witnessing was miraculous.

I think that his grandparents wanted to show him that dying is not something to be feared and that death would not separate him from his family, as those in spirit are very much around us and one day each of us will be reunited with our family and friends. They wanted him to experience their continued love and existence so he wouldn't feel so alone in the possibility of death. And they wanted to help him let go of his fear.

One day, however, I had a disturbing experience during a healing that had a huge impact on me. Jeremy was on his back on the healing table, and I was sitting at his head with my hands under his neck. My eyes were closed. I was taken to a scene where Jeremy was on his knees under an old, gnarly tree. Men were persecuting him for something he believed in and possibly something he had done. They were about to kill him. He had absolute terror in his eyes. The situation was filled with the darkest of energy; it felt truly evil. I saw myself, although separate from that circumstance, close to the scene, standing across a small stream from them. I held my hand out to Jeremy, pleading desperately for him to take it, as if I could pull him out of there. He did reach out and take my hand, and then, without further resolution, I was back in the healing room sitting at Jeremy's head. I wasn't sure what had happened—if Jeremy had got the help he needed, if I had been able to pull him out of there or not. I was terrified, and the energy had completely worn me out. I sat, trying to understand what this had been about. Was it symbolic of something in his present life, was it a past life, was it the cancer? I didn't know.

After about a week of healings, Jeremy was happy and feeling well, and he decided to go home. The day he left, as he packed a lunch and headed off to the airport with Jeff, he was a different person from the one who had arrived. Jeff and I thought he was healed. It certainly felt as though he was.

When Jeremy got home, he e-mailed me: "My belly feels great." I had urged him, when he got back to his mountain home, to spend some time in nature and meditate. I advised him to go slow and be calm and grateful, giving the healing a chance to work. I asked him to sit alone each day and bring the Universal light of healing through the top of his head and down through his body and send out love and gratitude in return.

But when I called Jeremy, he sounded busy and didn't seem too interested in sitting still in nature. Then I heard that Jeremy had decided to travel to Mexico for further treatment. From what I later understood, it had been a stressful trip.

Jeremy was gone for about a month. When he returned, he had a further blockage in his intestine and was having trouble eating. He called and asked if he could come back for another set of healings.

When he arrived, his fear had escalated almost out of control. Jeremy had become very angry and full of resentment; he said he felt a lot of shame for things other people had done. He wanted someone to blame for his cancer. He seemed to have shifted his energy into wanting others to take the responsibility for his cancer onto their shoulders. Blaming, while a very natural impulse, takes our power away from us. It makes us victims. The energy of being a victim is not great at any time, but especially not when we are healing.

But I understood where these feelings were coming from and I could sympathize with him. Jeremy was a police officer. He had chosen to go into the police force because he wanted to have a job where he could make a difference. He wanted to help and protect people. He was a deeply honourable person. I think because he was so honourable, he had been moved into a new position in the past year or so. He had been given the horrendous and difficult job of investigating his fellow officers who had engaged in inappropriate behaviour. Some of the things Jeremy told me were very disturbing. Every day, he was dealing with some of his co-workers who were choosing to live very low-vibrational lives, and was brought into constant contact with low energy. Not only that, but I feel he internalized his findings, keeping this energy stuck inside himself. This job also separated him from the team and made him feel alone. It was a stressful position, and I believe Jeremy wanted to do something different with his life but felt trapped by his ideas of what it is to be a responsible adult. His job, with its excruciating responsibility and utter lack of inspiration or joy, had lowered his spirit. He wanted to live from his heart and soul, but his circumstances seemed to control him.

Instead of the joyous and connected healings we had the first time, we spent hours talking, trying to work through all of Jeremy's anger and blame. But we did not seem to be making progress fast enough. Jeremy's fear increased steadily as he judged every healing to see if it had the same dramatic results as the first time. The pressure on me was intense; it was completely the wrong energetic environment. Jeremy was inadvertently blocking the love that was available to him.

Many times when I was talking to Jeremy, I felt as if I was channelling words from someone who was trying to help with the healing and was showing me images to demonstrate what was happening. I saw the energy from Jeremy's heart flowing outwards and then travelling back to him in a big loop. I wanted him to release these strings of resentment and shame, to sever them and focus instead on what he could send love and gratitude out to. It was clear to me how this energy loop was created and that he had to make the choice to go towards love. Anger will only make us weak, and by choosing it, we are hurting ourselves. So we need to make the effort to send out love. It can be to a tree, our grandmother, the Earth, the moon—just send out love. Get the flow going out from our hearts so that this higher-vibration energy can come back to us.

What I didn't really understand at the time was that I should have been healing Jeremy's heart chakra directly, and physically removing the blocked emotional pain that had built up there. Although the physical body heals the quickest, in the case of disease it is not where the true healing needs to take place. The energy that created the disease in the healthy body needs to be healed; otherwise, the disease will quickly reappear in one form or another. The disease is a symptom of a much more significant problem.

Jeremy decided to go home after a few days. He was consumed with fear and panic, and didn't feel the healings were moving quickly enough.

About a month later, I decided to fly out and see Jeremy at his home. He seemed much more relaxed and calm, but he was thin and weak. Once a day, he was getting liquid nutrients at the hospital via a tube into his stomach, and he was experiencing constipation, one of the side effects of the chemotherapy drugs that were being administered to ease his suffering. Although we did not talk about it, he seemed to have quietly accepted the thought of dying.

He was with his wife, daughter, mom and dad. We did healings every day for about a week. They felt like transitional healings, bringing a little more peace and comfort to Jeremy at the end of his physical life. By the time I arrived, it seemed he had already chosen to move from a place of fear, anger, and blame to one of love and appreciation. These healings were mostly a time for family and friends to come through from Spirit and give him messages. Although Jeremy was very good at connecting with Spirit, he told me he could only do so when I was with him.

I think his experience with Spirit and being able to communicate with his deceased grandparents created some of the most powerful healing that Jeremy received. It gave him the knowledge that the love of our family and friends lives on. It shone a light on the wonderful relationships he had had in his life. Much to Jeremy's credit, he took their message and allowed himself to heal on an emotional level in his personal life. It was wonderful to see him live in the moment and enjoy the little things that life had to offer. His dad told me about an evening they had shared recently when the two of them sat outside the hospital and watched the most incredible thunder-and-lightning storm. He said Jeremy just looked at him and smiled. A connection of love was felt, and words were not needed.

The healing that Jeremy didn't get was a release from the powerlessness and agony he felt in his position at the police force. He had witnessed so much conflict and abuse of power but was unable to resolve these situations before he was overcome with cancer. As in the vision I had observed, his life was being taken through the injustices of others. If it was a vision of a past life, then it seemed he hadn't healed the emotional pain from that lifetime.

Jeremy lived his life with the determination to act responsibly, doing what he felt he must for the sake of others. He was working to make the world a place where people would be more sensitive to and compassionate about the needs of others.

THE ENERGY WE CARRY

A N EXERCISE I sometimes do with people who come for healing is to ask them to see themselves objectively on their journey through life. I have them sit or lie quietly and imagine their soul has risen above their physical body and they can see themselves down below. I then ask them to witness their experiences through their life, from their first memories to the present day.

Our experiences can greatly affect us emotionally. Loving and kind encounters can empower us, while hurtful encounters can weaken us. If we attach ourselves to these emotions, constantly linking ourselves to them with the energy of our thoughts, we carry them with us on our life's journey. If an experience is hurtful and of a lower frequency, it's like putting a heavy weight on our shoulders or back and deciding to carry it wherever we go even though we are damaging ourselves.

We will always encounter people in very different stages of emotional development, and we will be hurt along the way. But we have the choice to keep ourselves connected to that pain, carrying it with us, or to put it down and lighten our load. By attaching ourselves to that lower-frequency energy, we directly affect our own energy field. Our thoughts are like ropes we throw around these packages of pain so that we can haul them with us. Visualize yourself walking along your path of life. If each time you have a hurtful encounter you take it with you, even though it weighs you down and keeps jabbing into you, you will inevitably become weaker as you carry on.

For me, forgiving means recognizing that people who hurt me are on their own paths and that there is nothing to be gained by constantly reinforcing my connection to their emotional experiences. Forgiving is letting go of or putting down that weight for my own benefit. I think I sometimes used to feel that if I held on to the emotional pain, I wouldn't be as vulnerable to getting hurt in the future; I'd be more aware. But really, holding on just holds you down, because the other person's slower energy is literally a drag on your own energy.

Forgiving is not the same as forgetting. When you put your finger in the fire and get burned, you don't then forget and keep putting your finger in the fire, allowing yourself to be re-burned. Similarly, forgiving has nothing to do with continually accepting painful behaviour into your life. It does not mean putting yourself in a position to be repeatedly hurt by someone who is not ready to change. By putting down the weight of the undesirable emotions, you are cutting the link between the emotions, the person who brought them into your life, and yourself. You are also allowing that person the opportunity to make better emotional choices in the future. You are not energetically holding them in the same place, but permitting them to shift to a higher place if they are ready.

Do not keep yourself tethered to the pain, but walk on, unencumbered. Do this for your own sake and your emotional well-being. Try to surround yourself with people who are working at making positive choices in their own energy patterns.

We may also do things that we regret or feel guilty about. Hopefully, we learn in the course of our own emotional development and choose to evolve. We are living in order to experience the consequences of our choices and expand our consciousness. We will only weaken ourselves on our journey if we carry the burden of guilt or regret. This does not mean forgetting our behaviour and repeating it, but learning from it and choosing to move to a higher frequency of emotional choice. By visualizing ourselves carrying these emotional weights, we can easily see the futility of doing so and appreciate why we should put them down and walk on in the creation of our own freedom and lightness.

LISTENING TO SPIRIT

Brad

ALTHOUGH EACH NEW step in my exploration of healing energy is exciting, as I never know where it will lead, I admit that sometimes fear sits on my shoulder. I try to use the fear to my advantage. I let it remind me that I feel vulnerable when I sense a healing is going to move up to another level. Acknowledging my fear pushes me to be extremely sensitive to any shifts in my awareness and to know that the success of the healing equals my degree of trust in something I don't necessarily understand. I am forced to surrender completely to the unknown, because only in the unknown can I move to the next level. I lean into my trust, nod to the fear, and let it go.

There is no formula for a healing. No two are alike, not even with the same person. From the moment I start, I have to let myself go, acknowledging that I have no idea where it will lead. I need to remain very sensitive to what I'm being told or shown. I'm in an altered state of awareness, the communication is subtle, and I rarely understand what it's about at the time. I'm being taken through the steps, but I'm not sure where we're going—other than, of course, to the ultimate goal of healing.

Brad's healing demanded that I completely trust from moment to moment. As Brad lay on the healing table, this is what I knew: He had a very serious heart condition and his doctors had not been able to find a treatment for him. His heartbeat was so irregular that he was, for the most part, confined to bed. The day he was first scheduled to come for healing, his wife called to cancel because she had to rush him to the emergency room. She drove him to my place the following day. They were both becoming very stressed.

So, going in, I was fearful. I had no idea what the healing would be about or what I was going to do. I had to trust that Spirit and this great Universal Love would come through, because Brad and I were completely depending on them.

I rarely get messages before I start. With Brad lying on his stomach, I placed my hands on his back. I closed my eyes and gave gratitude to the spirit world and to Source energy for the healing they would bring through me. I moved my right hand around just above the fabric of his shirt, waiting for my hand to start to tremble and connect with the energy. My hand responded quite quickly and started in with different patterns of movement. The healing began with an overall clearing of Brad's energy, removing surface irregularities in it, preparing us to go deeper.

I never talk during healings, because in my altered state of being, talking is not comfortable or natural. But not long into this healing, I was told that I needed to give Brad messages because there were things he needed to hear so that he would be able to let go of blocked energy and clear the way for the healing to be most effective. With that, my conscious self came in, fear right there in step. I felt uncomfortable giving messages during healings. What if I got them wrong?

But then I heard, "Tell him that it's not his fault."

My mind started to get in the way and I knew that wasn't good for the healing. *What's not his fault? What did he do?*

I heard it again, like a recording: "Tell him that it's not his fault."

It was a standoff between the messenger and my fear. My higher self urged me to side with the messenger. I said, "They're telling me it's not your fault—over and over, they are telling me that it is not your fault."

All this time my hands kept moving, patting, circling, clearing. Next I heard, "You are a good man. Tell him he is a good, good man."

The emotions I felt as I heard this were immense and I didn't know why. As the healing continued, I sensed a First Nations person coming in. Once again, my mind quickly interrupted. Was this a past life? I mentioned the person to Brad. I saw a totem pole along Brad's spine, a crossbeam along his arms. I had a sense of great strength coming from this First Nations influence.

I was now working on Brad's shoulder, my hands moving quickly and strangely. The main part of the healing seemed to be taking place here. I wondered what this had to do with his ailing heart. The intensity here was almost more than I could bear. It felt as though a weight of sadness was being removed. I cleared and pulled out, cleared and pulled out, what felt like endless ugly energy. Then it was gone. Coming back down Brad's back, I had an image of him standing, strong and whole, on an open, grassy hilltop, the wind blowing against him. He looked free and peaceful. A red-tailed hawk glided in the sky above him.

Then I began to feel someone's Spirit energy gently moving into my energy body. I felt I could trust this person. So even though this was very new for me, I gently stepped aside to let her use my form to connect to Brad directly. She didn't want to tell me something to relay to Brad on her behalf, she wanted to extend her love directly. Maybe it was a much stronger link if she could bring her energy into my energy field. For me, I felt as if I was this other person. And with this, I moved into her world and her thoughts and emotions. I was someone who cared for and looked after Brad. I saw Brad as a little boy. I loved him so much; I wanted to hold him and take care of him. Protect him. I felt as though I was sitting in a rocking chair, holding him in my arms. He was just a child. A sweet and innocent child. I felt this wondrous love and then became aware of this Spirit lady pulling her energy away from me.

I slowly returned to myself and saw Brad on the healing table. We were both crying.

I didn't know what much of it was about, but I was feeling relief, joy, and great love. I felt an overwhelming love in the room, an enormous love, beyond measure. And it was all there for Brad. Spirit and Universal Love came through in ways beyond what I could have hoped for or imagined. They came with a knowing of all things and an ability to heal because it was perfect energy of the most powerful love.

For this healing, I needed to go into the abyss, with trust and faith that the healing would be taken care of. My fear of my own shortcomings made me push myself to be the very best that I could be.

After the healing, Brad told me that his father had been very abusive, both physically and emotionally. Brad had been able to find protection in the home of an elderly First Nations woman and her husband. She had loved and cared for him as he was growing up, and had been the only person who could stand up to Brad's father, whose aggressive behaviour and large stature were no match for the spirit of this lady. This couple had been the guiding light in Brad's young life.

Brad's healing took place that day. The horrific emotions he had experienced as a child seemed to have accumulated in his shoulder, and after years of remaining there unreleased, they were affecting his heart. The energy of the heart chakra needs to be at a certain frequency for a healthy heart. Left unchecked, emotions from pain and suffering—insecurity, worry, blame, anger, hatred, powerlessness, insecurity, despair, fear, and so on—will affect the health of the heart or the flow of energy regulating the heart chakra.

This was one of the most amazing healings I had experienced, because Spirit energy came in so powerfully right from the start. There was no buildup with foundational healings; we just went straight in and got it done. I am forever grateful that I spoke the words I was given, because without them the healing would not have been complete and I would not have understood what had taken place. This healing deepened my understanding of the significance of the heart chakra and how critical our emotional well-being is to our overall health.

Brad's healing took place in about an hour, but his physical body took the time it needed to mend. Just as there is recovery time after surgery, physical healing takes the time the body needs.

Brad is now back to his normal life. He is planning to take some time, now and again, to think of his wonderful childhood guardians and send them love and gratitude, for not only did they come through for him when he was a child, they came through for him when he was a man, both times helping to save his life.

SPIRIT TAKES IT UP A NOTCH

Pat

HADN'T DONE A healing in quite a few months, choosing instead to concentrate on writing. But when Pat called and said he was in need of some energy work, there wasn't any doubt I would help. Within a few days, Pat was with me in the Centre. It was years since he had first come for healing and I really appreciated the respect he showed for the process. It was always beautiful to work with him.

Pat was very much in need of a change in energy. He said that he felt his life force energy was very low. I didn't understand what was causing this, but I knew the route to healing is not always clear and I could take only one step at a time. Pat had been diagnosed with a hiatus hernia, but when I meditated on him, I clearly felt this was not the main problem. We had to proceed and see what happened. At first I thought it was a few different things, none of them too serious. But as the days passed, the depth of the situation unfolded on a need-to-know basis. I was led by the energy of the healing and by Spirit in an order based on the complexity of the situation.

For the first couple of days, we worked all over his body. We spent a lot of time on his back. The blocked energy appeared in my mind's eye as dark brown and layered on his upper back. It felt unpleasant, like something you wanted to clean off and get rid of. I found it on the first day, and removing it was quite strenuous. Moving quickly, with a lot of intensity in my hands, I felt a little overcome at times by the type of energy I was dealing with. At one point I called out in my mind, asking if someone would please come and help me. At that moment I saw Hazel smiling at me. She held what looked like a coal scoop in front of a small round stove with a bright fire inside. As I cleaned the brown energy off, Hazel scooped it up and threw it into the fire. Having Hazel there and our fantastic teamwork gave me a lot of moral support. This type of energy removal can be very overwhelming and difficult to sustain. However, it appeared that Hazel found it no big deal; in fact, she looked almost to be having fun. This made all the difference to me.

Over the next week, we worked on Pat's neck and back. There were also the problems with the hernia, extreme acid reflux (which had no doubt contributed to the esophageal spasm that had brought him to me in the first place), and an irritable intestine and bowel. One day when he was lying on the healing table and I was standing beside him working with the energy over his intestine and stomach area, I saw the image of someone sitting beside me with their hands cupped around a spot over his intestine. My first thought was that I was being shown something I had to do later in the healing. But then it seemed that the figure was a spirit working independently on Pat. This was the first time I had sensed this so clearly in a healing. I had seen spirits before and had messages from them for the people I was working on, but this was the first time I saw something happening to a patient that wasn't directed by me. It felt odd, to say the least, but also necessary and important to the healing, so I carried on with my own energy work and the spirit continued to do what it needed on Pat's intestine. It sounds weird when I write it now, but it seemed part of the process in the moment.

Then, on our second-to-last day, we decided that the one remaining concern was the headaches Pat continually felt on the right side of his head. He attributed them to two accidents in the distant past: he'd suffered a concussion when his head struck and splintered a windshield in a car crash, and his cervical spine had been damaged by a heavy-lifting injury.

I decided to direct the healing energy to the right side of his head as I sat across from him. The energy, as usual, went in through the crown chakra in the top of the head. As it entered, it started making two-dimensional pinwheel patterns on the inside of the right side of his head. Then the pinwheel inverted and went inwards like a cone. As I watched, something—it may have resembled tweezers, but I didn't have a clear picture—entered the cone and took out what reminded me of an apple seed. When we finished the healing, Pat said his head felt better, with only a small remnant of the headache remaining. He went outside and spent the day in the sunshine, and it seemed he was doing well.

The next day was the last of our healings, as Pat had business to get to in Vancouver. But, much to my disappointment, when he got up in the morning, he had a terrible headache. It was by far the worst it had been since he'd arrived, affecting his vision and making it hard for him to walk. He made it out to the Centre and we started the healing on his head right away. As I directed the energy into his head, it looked as if something erupted in a burst, leaving a messy edge around the hole. I went behind him and started moving my hand around in circular motions. I sensed the presence of a spirit behind me and I felt he had his hand on mine and was helping to work on Pat's head.

After that, I told Pat to lie on his back on the healing table. As I stood behind his head, I felt myself getting very tired, as if I had been sedated. I kept hearing over and over in my head that I should go and sit down, and I got the impression I wasn't needed at the healing table. And so, not understanding what was going on, I went and sat down. I then felt a heavy pad being placed on my chest; it reminded me of the lead apron the dentist puts on you when taking X-rays of your teeth. I felt that it was being put over my heart chakra to protect me.

This was all very different from anything I had ever experienced before. I was, it seemed, to be an observer at this point. It was surreal: in my mind's eye, I was watching some sort of energetic surgery being performed on Pat. And whatever this spirit surgeon, as I'll call him, was going to take out of Pat's head was dangerous enough that he was trying to protect me from it. I knew I needed to let go of anything holding me back in my mind and allow whatever it was to happen.

As soon as I sat down, I saw in a vision three long, thin rods being inserted into Pat's head—one in the top and one in either side. I had no idea what these were for. Then I saw a long cut being made along the side of his head. Some thick black liquid flowed out, followed by a brown, mash-like substance. The visual image was not pleasant, but it was manageable. The sensation I got from that material, however, was very upsetting, almost more than I could bear. I had the image of a tall, dark figure walking away down a hallway. It looked like the back of a man wearing a long black coat. I felt completely unnerved by it, and I now understood why the lead apron had been placed over my chest. I don't know what this disturbing scene represented. Perhaps it was a very low-frequency energy being removed with the spirit healing.

When it felt as though the procedure was over, I had the urge to run from the Centre. But it seemed critical that Pat be covered in protective energy like a bandage until he was healed from the procedure and found his strength. I hugged him as he lay on the table and told him to be careful and to protect himself from external lower-vibrational energy. I asked to have white protective light all around him, and then I left and went to my bedroom.

I lay on the bed and cried; it was hard to cope with the powerfully low feeling of the energy that had been released. Jeff came to check on me, but I couldn't talk to him. He kept asking me to tell him what had happened, but there was no way I could talk about it. There are no words to describe what I felt; it was like nothing I had ever encountered in my world.

Later, I sat outside, trying to understand what had gone on. Pat is a kind, gentle person and this energy that came from his head was not of him. It felt like something foreign, but I was not sure what. Was it some sort of sinister entity that had attached itself to Pat? Because he is such an open person, perhaps this low-energy being had been able to lodge itself within Pat's energy field, taking his life-sustaining energy from him. It did feel as if this type of energy would have had harmful consequences if it had not been removed; maybe it would have become a brain tumour. I really do not know, but that is what it felt like to me.

Pat came in a little later and had some lunch. He said he was very tired and needed to go to bed. I knew he would require a lot of time to recover, because he had been through a great ordeal that would make him weak for a while.

He slept until the evening and then came outside to where Jeff, Logan, and I were sitting. Pat said that his headache was gone. He said he had had a feeling of something being drained from his head and that it now felt lighter. He thought that maybe it was his sinuses. This was the only thing that made sense to him.

The next morning, Pat was leaving for Vancouver. We went back out to the Centre for one last energy check-over. As I sat facing him, I scanned down his body, starting at his head, and asked how each part was. I would see the image of a word, such as "good" or "fine," written over each part of his body. It was a relief to get the message that his head seemed to be healed.

The experience of Spirit working directly on a patient, with my role being that of a coordinator, required a great deal of trust and faith in another reality far beyond my comprehension in the physical. This is not easy for me. For some reason I think I would be able to get my head around it more easily if it were someone else's experience and they were telling me about it. But for me, in my life, it was startling. Although the healing happened quickly, without a big buildup, the recovery for both Pat and me was quite long. I found it difficult to get over the images I had seen. But as hard as it was for me to deal with the energy, I was honoured and grateful that Spirit had felt I was ready for this level of healing. I want so much to measure up to my potential. It left me wondering what was next.

A NEW LEVEL OF HEALING

Pat

AFTER PAT LEFT, I felt that his healing process was not over. I kept thinking about him and trying to decide if I should call and say that I wanted to do more healing, but this time it would be focused on the heart. When I did call, Pat agreed that the healing did not appear to be complete, as he still did not feel like his old self. But now it was more a problem of depression. The prolonged cycle of fighting recurring illness and injury had taken its toll.

Depression is a broad label. It can include a lack of energy, a lack of zest for life, and loss of inspiration overall. The sparkle within is hidden away. Most people who come for healing are struggling with some form of depression but either aren't acknowledging it or don't seem to be aware of it as such. Therefore, the healings concentrate on the physical problems, and emotional healing takes place on the body wherever the blocked emotional energy presents itself. Except for the healing with Brad, I had never before been guided to the heart chakra as a main focus of attention. Now I would be shown the need to clear and heal the heart chakra's energy in order to allow the flow of energy that is required to truly heal one's body, mind, and soul.

Before Pat arrived, and in fact right up until the moment he was sitting in my healing centre looking at me, I hadn't the foggiest idea what I was going to do. I started by talking, hoping this might lead to something. Thankfully, I was given some information, possibly by one of his spirit guides. It was a brief message that although he was at an age when some people retire, he was actually meant to be doing more. He had spent the first part of his life learning a great deal about people from around the world, and he had acquired many unique perspectives on the Earth. Now it seemed he was meant to take his accumulated knowledge and do something inspirational for himself and meaningful for others. There was a sense that maybe he believed he had achieved most of his goals, but Spirit was saying to him that he had much more to offer the world and his soul had unfulfilled plans.

On the second day, I decided to sit opposite Pat and start by bringing energy up through his chakras. As soon as I began the healing, I had a sense of his mom and dad being present. They wanted to let him know that they loved him very much and had loved him all his life, even though they hadn't expressed it well. They placed a hollow glass cylinder in front of Pat and started to fill it with love for him.

After this part of the healing, Pat told me that he had felt connected to the area around his heart and had sensed layers peeling off it. Later, when he was on the healing table, I worked on his heart chakra. I was shown an image of a stalk of grass with grain blowing in the wind. It was viewed from a low angle from the perspective of the Earth. I did not know what this represented.

During the night before the fourth day of healing, I felt great excitement. I could sense spirits gathering, getting ready for the day's healing. I actually felt them lining up on the boardwalk to the Centre. I worked at getting back to sleep, as it was about three o'clock in the morning and I did not want to start interacting with them at that time. But I knew something was up—these people had a lot of energy and seemed very happy. When I got up, I detected a sense of anticipation and the spirits' desire to get going. We had breakfast, and the mood was so high from their wonderful energy that I wanted to head straight out for the healing.

When Pat and I sat down, facing each other to start the healing in the usual way, all I could do was laugh. These spirits were peers and friends from his life, eight to ten of them at least, and they were full of fun. The words I heard in my head just now—because one of them is here helping me write— were "They were full of piss and vinegar." I wouldn't say that myself—it's not the way I talk. But it is funny and true.

I decided to let them direct the healing. One of the men came through very clearly for me, and he turned out to be a close friend and kindred spirit of Pat's. They showered healing and love down upon us. There was a message to both of us that we shouldn't take everything so seriously and should have more fun, lighten up a little. I then saw the glass cylinder and they showed me that it was three-quarters full. Later on, when Pat was lying on the healing table, they showed me the image of a heart-shaped pillow that they were giving to him, with *Don't Worry, Be Happy* written in the middle of it. They had all signed their names around the edge.

It was a wonderful healing day, and I was left feeling full of life and so thrilled to be part of it all. At times during the beginning of the healing, I had felt as if I didn't really belong, like I was in a boys' club. I had the impression I should get them some beer and leave them to it. But I was needed to relay messages, and I was so glad I could attend. I felt that these guys were climbing friends of Pat's who had possibly passed in accidents, and having them come lightened some of the grief surrounding their deaths, replacing a measure of the sadness with love and laughs.

I was starting to make out a progression in the course of the healings. We had begun with love from a parental point of view. I realize now that the ground image with the grass signified starting from the ground up, with basic love. Then we went on to the love from colleagues and friends, and the cylinder kept filling.

The next day, Tibetan monks in robes surrounded the healing table. They seemed busy with a ceremony of their own. One sprinkled grains of something from a silver dish over Pat as he lay on the healing table. I wasn't surprised that this day was one of spiritual love. It made complete sense and felt so beautifully complete. The next day, the monks returned, and again they carried out their own healing.

I knew that the next day was our last day because it was all very still and it felt as if there was nothing left to do. I was shown the cylinder again and it was now overflowing.

In this set of healings, I was witness to something so magical. I was taken on a journey of the heart. I received a strong impression that this is a loving world we live in; we just have to find a way to rediscover it. I couldn't have imagined a more perfect week of healing. It all revealed itself and came together as if there were a plan. As I write this, it's been almost three years, and Pat says he feels like his old self again, happy and healthy.

I believe that I was shown a whole new dimension to the healing process, as well as our true connection in the bigger picture of our existence and evolutionary journey. In a way, it seems terribly simple, but then I don't think it's meant to be complicated. The simplicity and pureness make it so beautiful and honest. I do think this may be the keystone to a complete healing for the body.

This healing marked the beginning of great revelations for me, in seeing how it all comes together. I was so excited.

THE HEART CHAKRA

IT TOOK ME quite a while to appreciate the importance of the energy of emotion in the healing process. I under stood that our emotions have a great impact on our physical well-being, but I didn't see how the actual vortex of energy streaming through our chests was so critical not only to our healing but also to our continued health.

Many people call this energy vortex the heart chakra. What we call it does not matter, as long as we can understand its significance.

Seven main energy centres come up through the vertical centre of our body and head. The heart is in the middle, the fourth chakra up, and is the central energy of emotion. It connects the lower three energy chakras, which are with Earth energy, to the higher three energy chakras, which are with Spirit and Universal energy. I see the heart chakra and our emotions as the uniting energy between our body and our soul.

I believe the heart chakra is one of the most important aspects of our health. I have learned that unless the heart chakra is clear, either healing cannot take place at all or it will not sustain itself. The life force energy from the universe flows through us from our crown chakra at the top of our head, down through our other vortices of energy, and connects to our heart chakra. If our heart chakra is clear, then this energy can flow freely to the rest of our body. Our heart chakra is like an intersection of energy. The energy should be able to flow vertically and horizontally, optimally bringing higher energies of emotion from the world around us and from the higher energies connecting to spirit. But if lower energies of emotion accumulate in this vortex, slowing down the flow of energy, then it will be harder for us to thrive at an optimal level of health and well-being. The emotions we feel all have a direct impact on how well the energy flows through this area.

Our soul speaks to us through feeling, not thinking. Thinking and verbal language are adaptations of our physical form, but the voice of our soul through all of our existence is emotion. Feelings and emotions guide us through life and after we leave the physical form. Our true understanding of each other, the path of our lives, and our connection to Spirit will most successfully take place through feelings and emotions. Although thinking is necessary in the physical world for everything from learning about technology to paying our taxes, it cannot take the place of feeling as our greatest teacher. I believe that the power of our existence in the physical form has removed us further from our emotions and from being truly honest about them. Many times in life, facts on paper suggest a certain decision, but we have a strong inclination to do something else. This is our guidance system—our intuition, our higher self, and our connection to Spirit. We know, inside ourselves, what to do.

When we are stirred to feel joy, love, and passion, this is our soul leading us to the blueprint of our journey. These higher emotions guide us to a physical life of health and happiness. Learning to be guided by them not only leads us on the path we intended for ourselves when we came into this life and maintains our physical well-being, but it also guides us to a higher level of energetic frequency when our soul leaves the physical body at the end of this life. This energy, expanded from our spirit, will correspond to the frequency of energy we synchronize with when we cross from the physical form to the spiritual form. By choosing to follow our higher emotional feelings, we heed the voice of our soul and the calling of our evolutionary path.

Therefore, how evolved we are in terms of the emotions we are learning to use in our life experience not only has an enormous impact on ourselves but also influences how we directly affect the world. The vitality of the emotion we direct out to the world is returned to us; this is the frequency we resonate with, and it will flow with strength only if the heart chakra is not blocked by the slower energies of emotion. So this vortex of energy is our main emotional link to the world, both sending and receiving frequencies. The health of the heart chakra is like a message board for us. It's an indicator of the big picture of our life.

MARINA AND SAINT FRANCIS

ALTHOUGH I WAS excited by what I had learned about the importance of the heart chakra for healing and living, I continued to struggle with many of my experiences and found it hard to reconcile them with the everyday world. Some of the stuff I was seeing seemed so unusual and kind of weird. When I shared my struggles with Jeff, he told me to "embrace the weirdness." Jeff has always been fascinated by the unusual things I have seen and experienced. While he was able to readily accept them into his world view, sometimes it was harder for me.

My heart definitely pulled me towards writing this book, but because of its deeply personal nature, most of the time I didn't imagine I would ever publish it. But then, over time, a lovely combination of circumstances made me think I should try. I have no doubt that Spirit places opportunities in our path to help and guide us on our journey here on Earth; we just have to decide which opportunities we want to grasp.

This series of events started ten years ago when I was at the Arthur Findlay College in England. I was having a reading with a renowned medium named Eileen, an instructor at the college who is very finely tuned to Spirit energy. During the reading, she recommended that I do two things, both of which, she said, would help me understand my life. One was to read Paramahansa Yogananda's book *Autobiography of a Yogi*, and the other was to travel to Assisi in Italy and "walk in the footsteps of Saint Francis." Buying Yogananda's book was easy—I found it in the gift shop at the college. But travelling to Italy was a real stretch. I couldn't imagine how Jeff and I would ever have the money or the time to make such a trip a priority in our life. As intrigued as I was by what I might discover in Assisi, I felt that a trip there would definitely have to be put on the back burner.

My life moved along and was very full. My kids were growing up and our filmmaking business was getting busier. The healings were taking up more and more of my life. With all that was going on, I didn't think much more about Eileen's reading and its interesting message. Then, four years after that message from Spirit, things began to fall into place.

Marina, Giorgio's sister, and her husband, Pippo, came to stay with us at our home in Canada. They were filmmakers living close to Rome. We had become friends through Giorgio's healings, and our film-producing lifestyles gave us even more in common. They wanted to make a film about Jeff, Chelsea, Logan, and me and our life in the wild. So, in the summer of 2010, we invited them to share and document our lives. As their visit approached, I started getting a lot of messages from Giorgio. He really wanted me to arrange a reading for Marina with a medium. He wanted a chance to communicate with her. When Marina arrived, I asked her if she would be interested. She was incredibly excited. She said she had been talking to Giorgio in her mind and had recently said, "Giorgio, find a way for us to have a talk. You always found a way."

Marina told me that when they were children, Giorgio had set up tin-can phones on a string so they could try talking between their bedrooms. As they got older and lived farther apart, he always made sure they connected through e-mail and cellphone calls, and he later introduced her to Skype.

I decided on a phone reading from my house with Bernie in England, the medium who had connected with Giorgio years before. It worked out incredibly well. Marina had a wonderful reading, receiving serious information regarding business and some humorous messages. Giorgio told Marina to let their mother know she could quit praying for him now. He said he was all "shiny and clean," and she didn't need to worry about him. Marina confirmed that her mom prayed for Giorgio every day. Overall, Giorgio sent his love to Marina, trying to assure her he was still close.

But Giorgio wanted to create more ways to keep his love and those he loved united. He came to me and showed me a ring that I had kept tucked away in my jewellery box for many years. It was a gold ring with a tiger's eye stone. Although I had always thought it was lovely, I never wore it. I put it on a few times, but it didn't seem to suit me and I always took it off. Giorgio asked me if I could give this ring to Marina as a gift from him, something she could wear that would always remind her of his love. When I gave Marina the ring, she was very pleased and moved by Giorgio's desire to keep their relationship alive. The ring fit Marina perfectly and she loved it. It was as if I had been entrusted to keep this ring safe through the years until this moment.

The next message Giorgio brought to me was his thought that Marina and I could adopt each other as sisters. It felt like a wonderful idea to me and I hoped Marina would feel the same. She did not have any other siblings, so maybe a Canadian sister would do. I had felt a deep connection to Marina from the first time I met her in San Francisco. Within minutes we could talk about anything; we did not feel self-conscious or guarded, partly because we were meeting through Giorgio's healing and I was being my authentic self. There was clearly something special between us. And so, without reservation, I presented her with the offer of sisterhood, bound not legally on paper but within our hearts. Marina accepted immediately, joyful at the thought. With Jeff and Pippo present, we had a little ceremony at the Centre, joining our love together as sisters.

This sister bond developed even more meaning four years later and brought me full circle to the message Spirit had given me eight years before. Logan was very keen to study art after he graduated from high school. He researched all the art schools he could find and decided that the one that suited him the best was the Florence Academy of Art in Italy. I immediately felt that this was the right school for Logan, and I knew it was even more possible because Marina, his Italian aunt, would help with the logistics of moving and finding a place for him to live. Of course, Logan had to assume all responsibility for getting accepted into the school, which he did with flying colours. Having Marina in Italy took all the stress out of the move. I do not believe things like this are a coincidence.

In September 2014, Logan and I travelled to Italy to set him up in his new home. I stayed for a month, partly to help Logan with the transition and partly to have time with Marina.

While I was there, she suggested we travel through Tuscany and Umbria to Assisi. She said there was a retreat centre in the mountains near Perugia called the Ananda Ashram and they were putting on a three-day retreat titled "Walking in Saint Francis's Footsteps." Apparently Yogananda had travelled there from India to connect with Saint Francis's life and the ashram had later been built there.

I do not for one moment put myself in the same company as Saint Francis, but I was given the opportunity to visit the place where he had lived, to walk on the paths where he had walked, and to feel the expression of the land that had helped to create his love of nature and had inspired him to lead a life in pure love and healing. How could it be that I so effortlessly found myself exactly where Eileen had told me I needed to go?

Marina and I had a beautiful trip through the mountains and villages, winding our way up to the little sanctuary. We shared a room overlooking the forested valley. The ashram offered the perfect setting and people to help us on our pilgrimage. We visited the church Saint Francis had established and explored the area of Assisi. On our third day, we were given the privilege of journeying up the mountain that had been so sacred to Saint Francis. On this steep mountain were small trails where Francis had walked and places where he had meditated and contemplated. The cave that he had called home and the caves of his colleagues and friends were also here. Each was a small shelter of rock nestled in thick trees and foliage.

On our tour we were part of a small group of about ten people. Towards the end of the day, I found myself slightly separated from the others as they listened to the guide sharing historical information. I was so caught up in the magic of the mountain that I was less interested in absorbing facts.

Seeing me on my own, the other guide came over to be with me. She said, "I'm going to tell you something the others don't need to hear." She told me that it was in this place that Saint Francis had to make one of the biggest decisions of his life.

He loved nature, loved the animals, and loved being alone to fill himself with the inspiration of the Earth, the universe, and God. Could he justify a life of solitude or was it God's wish that he share his experience with the people in the villages below? He asked Saint Clare, a friend and follower of his, what he should do. After praying, she said that the message she received was that he was meant to go to the people. And so he did.

I was astounded that this guide had decided I should hear this story. Because in my own little way, on my own little journey, I was struggling to decide if I should share what I had learned and experienced. My love of nature, animals, and solitude made me question if I was really meant to try to publish my writing. But I am amazed at how the events of my life aligned to take me to the very place I was told to go eight years earlier so that I could receive a message that was incredibly meaningful to me at that exact moment.

If someone of the magnitude of Saint Francis questioned his direction in life, then none of us should be too hard on ourselves if our life's path is not always clear. But if Spirit keeps lining up our opportunities in a certain direction, maybe we should take note.

HEALING A PAST LIFE

Rob

SAT FACING ROB, tuning in to the energy on our third day of healing. Rob had come to me for a series of healings. He had been diagnosed with multiple myeloma, a cancer of the plasma cells in the blood. With my eyes closed, I scanned his energy field. Then, to his left, I got a glimpse of a passageway that I could look through. I found myself drawn down this passage, where I could see a young black man on his knees in terrible pain and agony. His wrists were tightly bound with rope. His suffering was unbearable to witness. Not only could I see his pain, I could feel his emotional trauma. I knew immediately that he was a slave and that I was seeing into a past life of Rob's.

It was unbearable and I wanted to pull back. I wanted out of this vision. It made me feel horrible. But I sensed that if I didn't go into this vision, energetically, and try to help him, we wouldn't be able to go further with Rob's healing. I knew that Spirit was giving me an opportunity to help in a way I had never been able to before, and I felt great trepidation.

From the moment I made the commitment to go forward, it was as if I was with that tortured man in that lifetime. Although I realized that I was not time-travelling, it felt as though I had stepped through a portal into his world, like I was standing in front of him as he knelt on a floor. He looked directly at me. His face is as distinct to me now as it was in that instant. His skin was smooth and clear. His eyes were kind and full of grace. There was something about his face, his energy, that made me feel so much love for him. I knew immediately that I had to untie the ropes that bound his wrists. They were the source of his intense suffering. I quickly reached out to untie the knots. The rope was thick and coarse. I fumbled with the knots and eventually managed to release them. He pulled his wrists free of the rope, and as it dropped away, he slowly stood upright, releasing his cramped muscles. How long he had been bound here was hard for me to imagine.

Then my perspective changed. I was no longer with him. It was as if I was watching a movie clip, and I could see him walking up a slight rise of an open, grassy hill. I could see a golden light shining down on him. I kept sending him intense love. I thought of flowers and beautiful things around him. Then I saw an older women in a flowered cotton dress come out of a little house that had a lovely old-fashioned porch across its front. She walked to meet this young man and put her arms around him. I knew in an instant that she was his mother. Her face was full of love as she held her son and looked up into his face.

I felt then that the energy of his life had been shifted. As I pulled my energy back from this man, I opened my eyes, returning to my healing room and to Rob sitting in front of me.

Rob said, "I don't know why, but my wrists are really sore." And at that moment his hands suddenly started to flip wildly around. From his elbows down, he had no control over his limbs. His lower arms and hands were twisting and flipping up and down. He reached up with his left hand and grabbed hold of his right arm, trying to force the motion to stop, but he couldn't. His arms and hands continued to move up and down, over and over.

I was scared. My heart was pounding. I felt I had unleashed something that I couldn't handle. My first reaction was to run to get Jeff, because I believed I was in over my head. But instead, I moved closer to Rob's chair and reached out and took hold of one arm and then the other. I steadied them, sending love and healing. I kept telling them, "It's okay, it's okay." Finally his arms and hands began to calm down. When they stopped moving, Rob started to laugh. He laughed and laughed as he hadn't laughed in a long time. This had seemed like such an intense and traumatic experience to me, and I was really scared there for a moment; I couldn't believe that Rob's first response was to laugh. And it wasn't a light chuckle—it was a deep and heartfelt laugh. It made me feel better too, just watching him.

Rob said, "I didn't tell you this earlier because it didn't seem connected to anything, but yesterday my wrists started aching." It seemed that Spirit had been preparing Rob for this part of the healing and for this experience. He said, "Last night, I awoke in the early hours because my wrists were hurting. I held my hand up and my skin appeared to be black—it was very startling. My hand looked like it was covered in soot. I never mentioned it in the morning because it just seemed so strange."

His emotional memory had already set the stage for our healing to take place. The way I see it is that the black man was never able to resolve his life circumstance of being a slave. He did not get emotional healing in his life. Maybe he died in slavery. The emotional energy of that lifetime was still part of Rob's energy. Later, Rob told me that he always felt as if he was carrying something from another time. He didn't understand it, but he said he felt he had an added burden in his life. I believe this painful energy had made Rob's life even more challenging and possibly even affected his emotional reaction to situations in his current life.

Sometimes we need healing in our present life to ease an emotional burden we carry from a past life. We may find it difficult to move forward with the complexities and challenges of our life when deep within our consciousness the energy of fear-based emotions still resides.

In order to free Rob up to allow his current healing to take place, we needed to heal his past life. I was shown this scene so that I could help bring in the higher frequency of love and change the energy of this memory in his emotional energy field.

THE HEALING IN CONTEXT

RECENTLY, AS I lay awake in bed at 2 a.m., unable to sleep in the dry August heat that filled the room, all I could do was think. The whirring of the fan couldn't keep up with the whirring of my mind. I was trying to summarize my experiences with healing so far and make sense of all the people I had worked with and the varied outcomes of their healings. All the people who had come for healings had experienced amazing energy and the most incredible love from Spirit, but quite a few had died. What was this about?

I am a person who looks at everything straight on, no matter how difficult or painful. Right from the beginning, realizing there was much I didn't yet know, I wanted to understand what was going on and be as honest with myself as possible.

When I started healing, my attitude was black and white: either these would be miraculous healings or I was not interested. I didn't even think about healing being a process of development for the person, an opportunity for their individual growth and emotional evolution. I saw it as a quick fix to personify the incredible power of these higher spiritual energies so we could demonstrate what was possible on a much bigger level. I cared deeply about each person, but I also wanted straightforward healings that could prove this energy existed. So it has been very challenging for me to come to terms with this much more complex picture of the human spirit and what our journey is about.

The situation was made even more troublesome for me because some people judged the healings harshly, without a true understanding of what was going on. But I didn't really mind this, because it gave me the incentive to question the healing even more deeply and pushed me to seek out the truth for myself. As much as I think we don't need answers for everything, I wanted to try to learn as much as I could; I didn't want to waste this tremendous opportunity I'd been given. But the people who were judging with a very limited amount of information were essentially onlookers with no grasp of the process. One was a doctor. This was interesting, because he judged the success or failure of my type of healing based on life or death. Yet if a doctor performed heart surgery and the patient lived but later died because they refused to change their diet, that doctor wouldn't feel that the surgical procedure had failed. And no matter how strongly the doctor might have advised the patient to quit eating cheeseburgers, if the patient wasn't ready to make that commitment, the patient's death wouldn't be put down to failure of the surgery. We all know the human condition is complicated, to say the least, and the issues most people are healing from are much more complex than deciding whether or not to eat cheeseburgers.

But still, I have gone over the healings where people later died and have had a really hard time accepting their deaths. Often, it seemed that choices made after the healings determined the person's experience. But in no way did that take away from the miraculous healing energy from Source. I feel that the healings mostly worked and did heal the person on at least the physical level at the time. On many occasions, MRI results showed changes; and at the time of the healing, many patients' symptoms had completely disappeared.

So what we can actually take from this is how complex our life's journey is. Our health depends not just on our own choices and experiences; we are also deeply affected by the people we share our lives with. I have seen this over and over. Our relationships with others teach us a great deal about ourselves and create situations for growth and understanding in our emotional development. But they can be very challenging and, sadly, can prove intractable at times. True healing requires a great deal of strength from a person, and their partner's attitude and support is a very important part of the process.

I believe that all of life is about healing. It starts at birth. We are healing right from the get-go with the energy we brought into this life. When we are born, we are the collective emotional energy that we have compiled from previous lives and from our time in spirit in between our physical lives. So as we begin our new physical life at birth, we are meant to continue our emotional healing process.

The circumstances we are born into and the level of emotional energy we are resonating with will obviously have a great impact on how onerous this healing will be. As we experience our lifetime, we constantly create healing opportunities for ourselves. I think disease is mostly a manifestation of healing left undone. We are each on our own path, and our healing requirements vary greatly. For some, the challenges are so overwhelming that finding healing may be very difficult. We can't compare our healing success with someone else's, because we are all in very different places on our emotional evolutionary journey.

Our life is a layering of many different types of energy that we have to try to navigate. And the healing energy of Spirit and Source exists at a whole other level. We can experience it and be greatly affected by it, but we are still the captains of our own ships. How we decide to move forward in our lives and what choices we make in our own healing are up to us. In life and in death, we are making choices.

The healings are not outside the person who is receiving them. They are not separate entities; they are an energy that we can infuse ourselves with when the time is right in our own soul's journey. The healings are a gift of beautiful energy, and the people receiving that gift can decide how they want to use it or if they want it at all. What they take from the healings may be exactly what they needed in this lifetime—and that isn't as simple as life or death. We are meant to start healing at birth, but the degree of healing is determined by a web of complexities, right up to our death. What might be considered a great accomplishment of healing for one person is different than for another, according to their individual paths and the energy surrounding their spirits. It is not for any of us to decide if someone else's healing was a success or not. My wish would be that they received what they needed, whatever the physical outcome might be.

I experienced an example of this recently. When I was living in Italy for a month, where Logan was attending art school, Marina asked if I could do healing with a woman who had been treated for ovarian cancer that was now spreading to other parts of her body. There was nothing else the medical system thought it could do, but I was open to helping her in any way I could.

She was a beautiful woman named Anna and she had a wonderful spirit. She was a mathematics instructor, and, as with Giorgio, I loved bringing together what many would think of as two different worlds—science and Spirit—but which I think are very much linked.

She came down to Florence and rented a little flat that we could use for the healings, which we did once a day for about ten days. The main room was very small, so we moved the table out of the kitchen and squeezed in a massage table in its place for the healings. Anna spoke little English and I spoke no Italian, so we used a lot of hand gestures and expressions to get our messages across. We called Marina to translate as needed.

Although I was skeptical of how the healing would work on someone who had undergone extensive chemotherapy, I was willing to see where it might lead. In the first healing I asked Anna if there was anything that had caused her pain in her past that she didn't really talk about. She said there wasn't. On about the third day, I saw three baby angels around her thigh area. They looked like babies with little wings. One was more prominent than the other two; I referred to this one as the "big baby" because it was bigger in energy. I didn't know Anna at all and didn't know if she had children. I felt that these were her babies in spirit, but wondered why there were three and why one felt bigger and more forward in its presence. The big baby moved up Anna's body towards her head and gave me the message that it completely accepted Anna's actions and, moreover, that it had only love for her. In fact, I got the impression the baby was a soul mate for Anna and was there to bring her love and guidance. This baby wanted Anna to know it was there for her with this enormous amount of love. They were kindred spirits for sure.

When I explained to Anna what I had seen, she told me that she had had an abortion when she was young. After that, when she was ready to raise a family, she experienced two miscarriages and had never been able to have children. The big baby was from the pregnancy she had terminated; the less assertive babies were the two she had miscarried. The one she had chosen to give up desperately wanted her to know that it had much love for her, and even though they hadn't had a physical life together, the baby had always been with her in a spiritual relationship. I also think it showed itself to me as a big baby because it was an old soul. This information was incredibly healing for Anna, who had locked up her feelings of guilt and loss her whole adult life. It was no wonder she had cancer in her ovaries; there was blocked energy there that had never been resolved. These messages from her spirit babies were what Anna desperately needed to hear.

The healings did not seem to stop the cancer. But for Anna, they were successful in healing one of the greatest emotional challenges of her life.

If our emotional evolution is what our life is about, then for Anna, moving from guilt and loss to love and acceptance was a great lifetime achievement. She also experienced the unconditional love of Spirit and learned that our relationships are far deeper than our physical manifestations.

Was this healing a failure because months later Anna passed from her physical life? I am sure it was not. But from the outside, without the knowledge of these intimate experiences, one might assume the healing was not successful.

What I saw in the beginning as so black and white, I now realize has many shades of grey. We are, each of us, on our own journey in this lifetime. The healing we need and experience is unique and personal. It is between us and our soul—it is not for others to judge.

WE ARE ONE

T USED TO be that when I heard someone say, "We are one," I didn't have a clear sense of what this meant or how important it is for us to visualize it. I think ultimately it is an expression of one of the most crucial aspects of our development, because understanding our connection is the beginning of the next level of healing for ourselves and for the Earth. I see the Earth as a living being giving the foundation of life to all of us who call it home. From the soil to the plants to the water to the air, it offers all animals—and that includes us—a place to thrive and grow. It is the most magnificent creation, with everything beautifully interwoven to sustain life physically, mentally, and spiritually. Its greatness is so profound that it is both humbling and an honour to be a part of this masterpiece.

The world can be recognized as shared or interconnected energy, and this brings us to oneness. Seeing ourselves as united naturally leads us to want to evolve our energy of love, compassion, and gratitude. The world seen only as the physical form of matter leads to the perception of separateness from each other. This in turn creates the lower frequencies of energy such as competition, greed, and fear, all of which are destructive energies. It is therefore important that we understand ourselves as energetic beings, all interconnected.

The way in which our energy is interconnected creates oneness, and not only with other people. Our energy is also interconnected with places and things, because they too have energy frequencies. We have a oneness with our environment and the animals and the planet. The emotional energy surrounding my body and mind intermeshes with the energy of those around me, as the energy surrounding you intermeshes with those around you. It literally travels from one body in waves and meets the energy waves coming out from another.

In a group situation, the energy can shift to a higher or lower vibration within the whole, rather than remaining separate with each individual. This is why you can feel your own energy change depending on who you are with. Large groups of people will feel or act in the same way because their personal energies are intermeshing and becoming one. The situation is even more complex when we take into account how the energies of our subconscious minds are connected. Therefore, as energy beings, we have great power when uniting our energy on a common front. We come together not just on an intellectual level but also on a tangible energetic level, with frequencies that can affect the physical world. This can have an impact on the energy nationally or even globally.

Through my years of healing and working with energy and Spirit, I have experienced how all energy is interconnected and how emotional and spiritual energy can heal our physical bodies. I know from this that it is also possible to heal the Earth. We are very powerful beings, and the future of the Earth and all life upon it depends on our choice of whether to evolve our emotional and spiritual energy. The same choices we make for our personal well-being are the choices we need to make for the well-being of the planet. As a species, we have lived in ways that cause destruction to the Earth and to ourselves because we are so delayed in our spiritual development. I say spiritual development because, to date, our choices as individuals and as a civilization have reflected fear more than love. To move up the evolutionary ladder, we have to shift to a place of love. What do we want our experience to be? And what part do we want to play in the future of our creation?

If we were to see every aspect of the Earth as if it were an aspect of ourselves, maybe we could better appreciate the effects of what we do. Either every choice is made from a place of love and compassion or it isn't. And if it isn't, we are choosing to stay in a place of suffering and destruction. If enough people choose to make a change, we can shift the balance of our energy frequency on the Earth to one of love.

Our survival, and the Earth's, comes down to whether we have the intelligence and comprehension to evolve on an emotional level. And this will be determined by our choices—the basic everyday choices we make in our lives. We need knowledge and understanding, because the choices we make in all aspects of our being can come together to heal the Earth.

I once met a retired university instructor from the United States who said there was "no hope"—no hope for civilization or the planet. He went on to say that every time he was a guest lecturer at a university and he found an empty blackboard, he would write in large letters across it "There is no hope." He had only one grandchild and he was gathering survival gear for her against the inevitable day, as he believed, when people finally completed the destruction of the Earth. This may sound extreme, but at least he was taking stock and feeling something.

Sometimes, when I look around at how so many people are complacent, living their lives without ever examining their impact on the world around them, I feel quite hopeless as well. But I think we live in a very interesting time, and many of us are in positions where we can make the decision to turn ourselves in a new direction; collectively, these decisions can have an impact on the overall health of the planet. Once enough energy is shifted to a higher frequency, the total balance will shift and the planet will begin to heal.

When I began to understand energy and healing, I felt I was being shown something much bigger than the healing of individual human bodies. Understanding how energy affects us personally is like looking at a smaller blueprint of how we affect the Earth and all that lives upon it. All the choices we make for our bodies—physically, emotionally, and spiritually— are interconnected and work to enhance or damage our own well-being, just as every choice we make affects the Earth and everyone else. I feel there is hope not only for us to holistically heal ourselves, but also for the Earth and our place in it.

What is good for the planet is good for us, and what is good for our country is good for us, and what is good for our neighbourhood is good for us, and what is good for our home is good for us, and what is good for our bodies and minds is good for us. We are not separate. We are one. The energy we experience will determine the levels of love, peace, and understanding or fear, suffering, and ignorance that make up the essence of our lives.

IT ALL COMES TOGETHER

JEFF AND I finally had a day together between filming trips. We were both a little tired and didn't feel like doing too much, but we wanted the day to be special. We enjoyed our coffee out on the porch in the morning sun. One cup turned into two—the beginning of a beautiful day. After breakfast, we decided to go out to the Centre. It is a very peaceful place, an ideal sanctuary for rejuvenating.

Jeff had remembered some healings I had done on a man twelve years earlier, shortly after we met Hazel and returned from England. Dana and Jeff had observed two of the healings and Dana had recorded what she was seeing as a medium. Jeff thought it would be interesting to listen to the tapes, as we could hardly remember what had happened. We found the second healing tape first. As it played, we lay on our backs on the carpeted floor. It was incredible what Dana had witnessed during the healing. She described such things as spirit doctors coming to witness what I was doing, the man's father standing quietly on one side of the room, and even an angel offering protection over the healing. We then wanted to find the first healing tape. All my recordings of various readings by mediums were piled in a basket; most were labelled, but some were just mysteries. We couldn't find the right cassette, so we started trying the unlabelled ones.

Jeff found one that had been stopped halfway through and hadn't been rewound. He popped it in to see what was on it. We heard a woman talking to Jeff and me. She was obviously doing a reading for us, but we couldn't remember who it was. She was talking about a healing I had done many years before on a woman named Karen, who had had breast cancer. Although I had heard this information many years ago, I had not been able to understand its significance until now.

The medium was saying that I was called to heal Karen on a much different level than the physical. She said that the cancer was irrelevant; what Karen needed more was a healing on the emotional front, in the emotional body. Her emotional body was in greater jeopardy than her physical one. Because, the medium said, even if Karen had a successful operation to remove the cancer lump from her breast, she still would never let go of the cancer. The reason the cancer had developed was deep within her emotional being. So I was called to do something that Karen was unable to do herself. It was successful, because she did let go of what was causing her physical illness on the emotional level.

I have, over the years, come to understand these ideas about healing and have learned a great deal about the importance of healing a person's emotional energy. It is one of the biggest aspects of my writing. But as I was listening to this woman's voice, a very clear message suddenly came into my head.

My purpose in this life is to help heal people's emotional energy and thereby to bring healing to the planet by helping people evolve on an emotional level. The information I have received throughout my experiences with energy has all led me to understand the great importance of healing the emotional body, as we are first and foremost emotional and spiritual beings. The healing of the emotional body comes back to the very essence of our emotional evolution.

This realization felt so clear and right. It was as if a huge weight had been lifted off me. I had been connecting the dots for the past seventeen years, and now I had connected my own dot with the rest. Before this, I had a pretty big picture about energy healing and how it worked, but now I could finally see my place in it.

Knowing that I was able to help people heal their emotional bodies was an enormous breakthrough in my understanding of my place as a healer. I have struggled since the beginning to understand myself as a physical healer, and I have always felt uncomfortable seeing myself in that light. But in the much larger scope of our existence, living from one lifetime to another, it's our emotional being that we are ultimately striving to heal. The physical body of one life is insignificant in comparison with the many lifetimes through which we carry our emotional energy.

Jeff and I later found the other tape we had been looking for, the first part of the man's healing. We listened as Dana described an energy being working behind me and moving my hands. She wasn't sure if it was my higher self or a form of pure consciousness. It came as a huge ball of light and then formed behind me as a being. Perhaps it formed as something Dana could see to help her understand what was happening. She said it looked as though I was in an altered state and wasn't aware of what my hands were doing. The being and I were emanating pink, which is unconditional love.

On the recording, Dana says, "I'm sure it's deeper than that, but from my perspective it looks like [Sue's] healing him with love. I know it sounds crazy, but that's what it looks like. I see the heart chakra, pink and just rays of pink, unconditional love coming out. It leads me to believe that what Sue is really giving off is unconditional love to such a huge degree that it comes from Source itself. It's so powerful. This being... there is absolute unconditional love. I wish people could see it, because I'm telling you, people would believe in God and people would believe in all things spiritual."

I have felt many times during healings that an all-encompassing love filled the room. Experiencing the sensation of this love and this extreme energy fills me with the conviction that the possibilities for our future are limited only by the restrictions we put on ourselves. For me, this love is the energy that comes directly from the highest source. Some would call it God, but what we call this love doesn't matter. It's an intentional love from a very high and powerful origin. It's a love that makes me believe everything is perfect and anything is possible, that there is unlimited abundance and that whatever we need is available.

BACK TO HAZEL

AZEL WAS THE catalyst I needed to open my pathway. First she let me feel safe as I discovered a place far beyond anything I had ever imagined. Then her cancer pulled from me a memory of healing that I, in my physical form, had no comprehension of. But just as importantly, from the first time I met Hazel, I felt that I had known her before. I was very comfortable with her as she taught me and guided me with all she knew and understood from her experience. I was able to love her deeply, as if I always had. Even though our time together in this life was limited, I knew her through and through. We met with much work to do. She was the combination of what I needed to open my soul to its memory, to allow me in this lifetime to reconnect.

This reconnection is like waking up with amnesia and then slowly remembering. When pieces of information appear, there is a knowing that they make sense, a recognition of the truth that I can't deny. I also know that Spirit comes with love and wisdom and words far beyond my earthly abilities and coaxes me along, guiding me and working with me to bring the truth of our existence to light.

What started with the unrelenting message in my mind, those nights as I lay in bed in England many years ago, that I was meant to do so much more in my life has led me on a journey of energy and understanding. The energy moving my hands and its wondrous outcomes have been the proof my mind has needed to continue. Bit by bit, the path has unfolded in front of me as I found the courage to continue. It has been seventeen years since I met Hazel. I have walked on since then, carefully and secretly, wanting to be certain at every new turn that I was staying faithful to my soul's truth.

All my life I've tended to hold my cards pretty close to my chest. But now I've decided to do one of the first things Hazel ever talked to me about. She said she was too old to worry about what people thought of her. While she still had time, she said, she wanted to share her experiences and help people through what she had learned. When I think about what a difference it has made in my life that Hazel was open enough to share her world view with me, I can't thank her enough. And I can't begin to imagine my life without her.

I've heard it said many times that when one door closes, another opens. But when the wind blew our door shut on that ordinary day, I could never have imagined where walking through Hazel's door would lead.

ACKNOWLEDGEMENTS

STARTED WORKING ON this book fifteen years ago. It's been a long journey and I would never have made it without the help of some very special people along the way.

To my mother, Irene Logan, I am so grateful that you always believed in me and had so much respect for the healing work I do, and for the many times you have told me how proud you are of me. I am also forever thankful that you gave me such an incredible appreciation for nature. I remember when I was six and we were walking in a meadow of flowers by a little stream, and as my joyful heart delighted in the beauty of nature, you gently told me, "This is your church." True to your word, it has always been my place of salvation.

To my uncle, Stan Logan, thank you for your incredible enthusiasm for my stories about my experiences while I have been on this spiritual path. Your respect, appreciation, and gratitude have been greatly appreciated. You have always been one of the best listeners I have ever known. Sharing your excitement and insights about what it has all meant was part of the reason I decided to write this book. "Far out!"

To my dear friend Charlie Russell, how much I loved our long and diverse talks on subjects ranging from bear energy to emotional energy to healing the Earth. I loved that you "got" the idea of my healings and respected them enough to introduce me to the wider world. We joked that you were my agent. Neither of us were ones to conform to society's rules, and we both sought our own truths in our fields. There was so much more overlap between the work you were doing with bears and the energy healing that I was doing than even we knew when this all started. Now that you have taken flight, I wish for your skies to always have "ceiling and visibility unlimited."

To Pat Morrow, thank you for placing your trust in me from the beginning. You are so well-travelled, with so much accumulated wisdom, I am grateful to glean insight from your life perspective. You've had many experiences with amazing healers around the world, from the Amazon to the Himalayas. I am humbled to have gained your respect and honoured to have shared my healing with you. Thank you for being the kind, gentle, and wonderful soul that you are.

To my dad, Jim Logan, I share your love of writing and I always appreciated your love of the mystical. My love to you, thanks for the dimes from heaven. xo

To Dana, thank you for sharing with me the messages of love and support that you received from the other side. You have always been one of the most gifted mediums I have ever had the privilege of knowing. You have shown me how much the spirit world has to offer us as we search for the signposts along our paths. Your friendship, love, and support on this journey have meant more to me than you can know.

Marina Cappabianca, my Italian sister, thank you for all your love over the years. Giorgio brought us together. It's another of his gifts to me for which I can never thank him enough. You are such a bright light of love and joy, and I can't thank you enough for all the support that you have given me over the years. I so look forward to our next journey together.

Sharon Zieske, my lovely friend, you were one of the first people to read an early draft of this book. You stayed up most of the night, reading and e-mailing me your reactions in the moment. It is one of my best memories. I was so unsure if I had anything to say and if my book would help people. Your unbridled enthusiasm and the joy you took in my story inspired me to keep going at times when I felt like giving it all up. Thank you for your continuing love and support.

Susan Fitzgerald, you were my first professional editor and I thank you for your kind and gentle approach to my work. I was so nervous about going out into the world with this story, but you made me feel safe and I thank you for that. You were always so helpful with suggestions and believed in my writing and its tone. You said reading my book was "like having a cup of tea with a good friend," and that's how I hoped it would come across, very approachable. I always felt you really understood me.

To Marcus, Tim, Elina, Jennifer, Leanne, Sharon A., Erica, Cathryn, Mehrnaz, Justin, and Jen, you all encouraged me with my writing. Thank you.

To my editor, Amanda Lewis, thank you so much for helping me to be clear with my story. Your detailed reading of my manuscript, your inspired notes, questions, and heartfelt comments made this book the best that it could be. You kept me engaged at a time when I was getting weary of this long process. Cheers.

To Trena White, co-founder of Page Two, thank you for taking the time to engage with my book and for giving me the opportunity to share my story. Thanks also to John Sweet,

Rony Ganon, Caela Moffet, Peter Cocking, and the rest of the Page Two team for helping me get this book out into the world.

The final and most important acknowledgements belong to my loving family.

To my daughter, Chelsea, my book wouldn't be here now without your love and support. You have been such a big part of everything I've done, from being my partner on healing trips to creating my first website and helping me organize retreats. You were one of the few people brave enough to read an early draft of my book and give me comments. You came back to me with detailed and honest notes. You had amazing insights and suggestions, and I was so grateful that you weren't afraid to be truthful. Your ideas were spot-on and I incorporated them all. We have shared so much through our lives together. The way you achieve your own goals is such an inspiration for me. I love you and admire you and thank you for always being there for me.

My son, Logan, you are wise beyond your years and I couldn't imagine going through this life without you. You are a cornerstone in my world. We have shared so much together, and throughout it all you have always shown generous and loving support for me and for what I have been trying to do. You were so enthusiastic and helpful with all your creative ideas for different book covers. I have such lovely memories of spending a month with you in Florence, me writing away each day in your little flat while you were at school, then sharing our thoughts through the evening as we sat on your tiny balcony with our wine and olives. You have been an inspiration to me to continue following my dreams and be unapologetically myself. Thank you, Logan, for helping me see the value of what I am doing and showing me the importance of following my own path.

You come into this world with people who are already part of your life—mother, father, grandparents, uncles, siblings. When you have kids of your own, they continue this long chain of family connections. But there is usually only one person with whom you knowingly choose to go through a lifetime. I couldn't have chosen a better life partner than my husband, Jeff Turner. You have been my rock through thirty-five years of marriage and I have never loved you more. Jeff, my writing, my healing, my connection to Spirit, and my ability to share my experiences with the world would not have happened without your undying love and support. You have always been the calm centre of my world. Early on in this journey, I was worried about how crazy some of my experiences seemed. I remember telling you this one day, about how I thought it all seemed just "a little too weird." And without hesitation or concern, you told me to just "embrace the weirdness." And I loved that. It was perfect. You believed in me, even when I was most in doubt about what was happening. You kept track of the big picture when I got lost in the details. You are on this journey with me, always walking by my side but also letting me find my own way. Thank you, Jeff, for everything you have done for me: all the big things and the thousands of little ones. My forever love.

ABOUT THE AUTHOR

SUSAN TURNER WAS born in British Columbia, Canada. She grew up in a small log home and attended a one-room schoolhouse, with her mother as the only teacher, from grades one to six. Her childhood was spent in nature, riding her pony and roaming the woods and mountains around her family's home with her little dog. Susan grew up with a profound love for the wilderness and the animals that live there, including bears, coyotes, cougars, and deer.

She and her husband, Jeff, met when they were fifteen. She helped him make Super 8 films throughout their high school years. Later, they were able to combine their love of nature and wildlife with their passion for making films when they got their first job working on a television documentary about black bears for PBS in the mid-1980s. Since then, Susan and Jeff have made over thirty different wildlife documentaries for the BBC, CBC, PBS, and the Discovery Channel. Their films have been seen in more than eighty countries. Susan and Jeff have two children, who started travelling with them to remote wilderness settings from the time they were five months old. The children went on to take their schooling by government distance education so the family could stay together.

At the age of forty, Susan unexpectedly discovered that she could connect to Spirit and had healing energy that came through her body and hands. For the past seventeen years she has been on a journey to understand what this healing energy means. She has come to realize how powerful our emotional and spiritual energy is—that it can help us not only to heal on many levels but also to understand our life's journey. Susan has made the connection between the healing energy she experiences and the healing energy that comes from the natural world. She has worked to help countless people experience healing in their mind, body, and soul.

To find out more, visit Susan at wildheartspiritheart.com